# CIMA

OPERATIONAL LEVEL

# PAPER P1

MANAGEMENT ACCOUNTING

XAM PRACTICE KIT

**FOR EXAMS IN 2017**

BPP
LEARNING MEDIA

Third edition 2016

ISBN 9781 5097 0706 5
e-ISBN 9781 5097 0739 3

**British Library Cataloguing-in-Publication Data**
A catalogue record for this book
is available from the British Library

**Published by**

BPP Learning Media Ltd
BPP House, Aldine Place, 142/144 Uxbridge Road
London W12 8AA

www.bpp.com/learningmedia

Printed in the United Kingdom by Wheatons Exeter Ltd

Hennock Road
Marsh Barton
Exeter
EX2 8RP

Your learning materials, published by BPP Learning
Media Ltd, are printed on paper obtained from
traceable, sustainable sources.

All rights reserved. No part of this publication may be
reproduced, stored in a retrieval system or transmitted,
in any form or by any means, electronic, mechanical,
photocopying, recording or otherwise, without the prior
written permission of BPP Learning Media Ltd.

The contents of this book are intended as a guide and
not professional advice. Although every effort has been
made to ensure that the contents of this book are correct
at the time of going to press, BPP Learning Media
makes no warranty that the information in this book is
accurate or complete and accept no liability for any loss
or damage suffered by any person acting or refraining
from acting as a result of the material in this book.

©
BPP Learning Media Ltd
2016

**A note about copyright**

Dear Customer

What does the little © mean and why does it matter?

Your market-leading BPP books, course materials and
e-learning materials do not write and update themselves. People
write them: on their own behalf or as employees of an
organisation that invests in this activity. Copyright law protects
their livelihoods. It does so by creating rights over the use of the
content.

Breach of copyright is a form of theft – as well as being a
criminal offence in some jurisdictions, it is potentially a serious
breach of professional ethics.

With current technology, things might seem a bit hazy but,
basically, without the express permission of BPP Learning
Media:

- Photocopying our materials is a breach of copyright

- Scanning, ripcasting or conversion of our digital materials
  into different file formats, uploading them to facebook or
  emailing them to your friends is a breach of copyright

You can, of course, sell your books, in the form in which you
have bought them – once you have finished with them. (Is this
fair to your fellow students? We update for a reason.) Please
note the e-products are sold on a single user licence basis: we
do not supply 'unlock' codes to people who have bought them
second-hand.

And what about outside the UK? BPP Learning Media strives to
make our materials available at prices students can afford by
local printing arrangements, pricing policies and partnerships
which are clearly listed on our website. A tiny minority ignore
this and indulge in criminal activity by illegally photocopying our
material or supporting organisations that do. If they act illegally
and unethically in one area, can you really trust them?

**BPP**
LEARNING MEDIA

# Contents

# Question and Answer index

BPP
LEARNING MEDIA

# Using your BPP Exam Practice Kit

One of the key criteria for achieving exam success is question practice. There is generally a direct correlation between candidates who study all topics and practise exam questions and those who are successful in their real exams. This Kit gives you ample opportunity for such practice throughout your preparations for your OT exam.

All questions in your exam are compulsory and all the component learning outcomes will be examined so you must **study the whole syllabus**. Selective studying will limit the number of questions you can answer and hence reduce your chances of passing. It is better to go into the exam knowing a reasonable amount about most of the syllabus rather than concentrating on a few topics to the exclusion of the rest.

Practising as many exam-style questions as possible will be the key to passing this exam. You must do questions under **timed conditions**.

## Breadth of question coverage

Questions will cover the whole of the syllabus so you must study all the topics in the syllabus.

The weightings in the table below indicate the approximate proportion of study time you should spend on each topic, and is related to the number of questions per syllabus area in the exam.

| P1 Management Accounting Syllabus topics | Weighting |
|---|---|
| A Cost accounting systems | 30% |
| B Budgeting | 25% |
| C Short-term decision making | 30% |
| D Dealing with risk and uncertainty | 15% |

# The Objective Test exam

The Objective Test exam is a computer based assessment (CBA), which is available on demand at assessment centres all year round.

Objective Test exams in each level can be taken in any order, but candidates must pass all the OT exams for a level before they can sit the Integrated Case Study Exam for that level.

Each exam lasts for 90 minutes and the pass mark is 70%.

Results are available shortly after the test has been completed, and the results will include feedback.

The exam will be made up of different types of questions, including:

| Question Type | Explanation |
|---|---|
| Multiple choice | Standard multiple choice items provide four options. 1 option is correct and the other 3 are incorrect. Incorrect options will be plausible, so you should expect to have to use detailed, syllabus-specific knowledge to identify the correct answer rather than relying on common sense. |
| Multiple response | A multiple response item is the same as a multiple choice question, except more than one response is required. You will normally (but not always) be told how many options you need to select. |
| Drag and drop | Drag and drop questions require you to drag a "token" onto a pre-defined area. These tokens can be images or text. This type of question is effective at testing the order of events, labelling a diagram or linking events to outcomes. |
| Gap fill | Gap fill (or 'fill in the blank') questions require you to type a short numerical response. You should carefully follow the instructions in the question in terms of how to type your answer – eg the correct number of decimal places. |
| Hot spot | These questions require you to identify an area or location on an image by clicking on it. This is commonly used to identify a specific point on a graph or diagram. |
| Drop-down list | Drop-down lists follow the same principle as multiple choice questions, in that you need to select one option from a pre-defined list. This can be used in conjunction with a gap-fill question: for example, you may be asked to key a numerical answer into a gap-fill box and then select an explanation for the approach you've taken from a drop-down list. |

BPP
LEARNING MEDIA

# Learning Objectives

The table below has been prepared by CIMA to help you understand the abilities that CIMA is seeking to assess.

| Learning objective | Verbs used | Definition | Example question types |
|---|---|---|---|
| **1  Knowledge** | | | |
| What you are expected to know | • List | • Make a list of | MCQ |
| | • State | • Express, fully or clearly, the details of/facts of | MCQ |
| | • Define | • Give the exact meaning of | MCQ |
| **2  Comprehension** | | | |
| What you are expected to understand | • Describe | • Communicate the key features of | Multiple Response |
| | • Distinguish | • Highlight the differences between | Multiple Response |
| | • Explain | • Make clear or intelligible/state the meaning or purpose of | Drop down list |
| | • Identify | • Recognise, establish or select after consideration | Hotspot |
| | • Illustrate | • Use an example to describe or explain something | Drop down list |
| **3  Application** | | | |
| How you are expected to apply your knowledge | • Apply | • Put to practical use | Multiple response |
| | • Calculate/ compute | • Ascertain or reckon mathematically | Number entry |
| | • Demonstrate | • Prove the certainty or exhibit by practical means | Hotspot |
| | • Prepare | • Make or get ready for use | Drag and drop |
| | • Reconcile | • Make or prove consistent/ compatible | Drop down list |
| | • Solve | • Find an answer to | Number entry |
| | • Tabulate | • Arrange in a table | Drag and drop |
| **4  Analysis** | | | |
| How you are expected to analyse the detail of what you have learned | • Analyse | • Examine in detail the structure of | Multiple response |
| | • Categorise | • Place into a defined class or division | Drag and drop |
| | • Compare & contrast | • Show the similarities and/or differences between | Hotspot |
| | • Construct | • Build up or complete | Drag and drop |
| | • Discuss | • Examine in detail by argument | Multiple response |
| | • Interpret | • Translate into intelligible or familiar terms | Multiple response |
| | • Prioritise | • Place in order of priority or sequence for action | Drop down list |
| | • Produce | • Create or bring into existence | Drag and drop |

| Learning objective | Verbs used | Definition | Example question types |
|---|---|---|---|
| **5 Evaluation** | | | |
| How you are expected to use your learning to evaluate, make decisions or recommendations | • Advise | • Counsel, inform or notify | Multiple response |
| | • Evaluate | • Appraise or assess the value of | Multiple response |
| | • Recommend | • Propose a course of action | Multiple response |

In your CBA, questions will be set which test up to the cognitive level of the verb in the component learning outcome in each paper's syllabus, so this means they will test up to level 5 verbs where the learning outcome permits this.

CIMA will limit the number of lower level questions in the exam – so that students will not be able to achieve the pass mark solely based on correctly answering knowledge and comprehension questions. Higher level questions, requiring candidates to demonstrate application, analysis and evaluation skills must be answered correctly for the pass mark to be reached.

BPP
LEARNING MEDIA

# Passing the P1 Objective Test exam

## Tackling objective test questions (OTQs)

- Read, and **re-read the question** to ensure you fully understand what is being asked.

- When starting to read a question, especially one with a lengthy scenario, **read the requirement first**. You will then find yourself considering the requirement as you read the data in the scenario, helping you to focus on exactly what you have to do.

- **Do not spend too much time on one question** - remember you should spend 1½ minutes, on average, per question

- If you cannot decide between two answers – look carefully and decide whether for one of the options you are making an unnecessary assumption – **do not be afraid of trusting your gut instinct**

- **Do not keep changing your mind** – research has shown that the 1st answer that appeals to you is often the correct one

- Remember that marks are awarded for correct answers, and marks will not be deducted for incorrect answers. Therefore **answer every single question**, even ones you are unsure of.

- Always submit an answer for a given question even if you do not know the answer - **never leave any answers blank**

- **Pace yourself** - you will need to work through the exam at the right speed. Too fast and your accuracy may suffer, too slow and you may run out of time. Use this Kit to practise your time keeping and approach to answering each question.

- If you are unsure about anything, remember to **ask the test administrator** before the test begins. Once the clock begins ticking, interruptions will not be allowed

- Remember to **keep moving on!**  You may be presented with a question which you simply cannot answer due to difficulty or if the wording is too vague. If you have only approximately 90 seconds per question, and you find yourself spending five minutes determining the answer for a question then your time management skills are poor and you are wasting valuable time.

- If you finish the exam with time to spare, use the rest of the time to **review your answers** and to make sure that you answered every OTQ

# Demonstrating your understanding of P1

The P1 examiner will expect you to demonstrate the following:

| Management accounting knowledge | P1 stresses the importance of costs and the drivers of costs in the production, analysis and use of information for decision making. You will knowledge of the whole syllabus. |
|---|---|
| Carry out appropriate calculations | You will need to perform calculations that relate to the scenario described in the question. |
| Make reasonable recommendations | The time focus of P1 is the short term. You will need to make short-term decisions, usually on the basis of calculations. |
| Understand risk | You will need to show an understanding of the impact of risk when making decisions. |

All OTQs in all the exams are worth the same number of marks, both in this Kit and in the real exam. However this is an approximate guide: some OTQs are very short and just require a factual selection, which you either know or you don't, while others are more complex, which will inevitably take more time. Note that the real exam will be balanced such that the 'difficulty' of the exam will be fair for all students – the OTQs in this Kit have also been balanced in a similar way.

## Using the solutions and feedback

Avoid looking at the answer until you have finished a question. It can be very tempting to do so, but unless you give the question a proper attempt under exam conditions you will not know how you would have coped with it in the real exam scenario.

When you do look at the answer, compare it with your own and give some thought to why your answer was different, if it was.

If you did not reach the correct answer make sure that you work through the explanation or workings provided, to see where you went wrong. If you think that you do not understand the principle involved, work through and revise the point again, to ensure that you will understand it if it occurs in the exam.

BPP
LEARNING MEDIA

# Objective test questions

BPP
LEARNING MEDIA

# 1 Modern business concepts

1.1 **Which TWO of the following are NOT features of a just-in-time (JIT) purchasing and production system?**

☑ Maximum capacity utilisation.

☐ Pull scheduling: buying or producing at each stage of the supply chain only when the next stage in the chain wants the output.

☐ Kanban control: using a system of signalling work flow requirements using cards or other signalling devices.

☐ Greater visibility of what is going on, such as open plan work place layouts and coloured lights to indicate stoppages.

☑ Relying on a wide range of suppliers for raw materials and components, to ensure immediate availability of items.

1.2 **CIMA's definition of just-in-time (JIT) production is:**

☑ A system which is driven by demand for finished products, whereby each component on a production line is produced only when needed for the next stage

☐ A system in which material purchases are contracted so that the receipt and usage of material, to the maximum extent possible, coincide

☐ A system where the primary goal is to maximise throughput while simultaneously maintaining or decreasing inventory and operating costs

☐ A system that converts a production schedule into a listing of the materials and components required to meet that schedule, so that adequate inventory levels are maintained and items are available when needed

1.3 Good quality saves money but the cost of quality can be analysed into cost of conformance and cost of non-conformance.

**Which one of the following costs is classed as a quality-related appraisal cost?**

☑ Re-inspection cost
☐ Administration of customer complaints section
☑ Performance testing
☐ Training in quality control

1.4 **Which THREE of the following contribute to successful implementation of JIT?**

☑ Close relationship with suppliers
☑ Minimal set-up time and costs
☐ Non perishable raw materials
☐ Non perishable finished goods
☑ Similar production time across all stages of the production process

1.5 **Which THREE of the following are arguments against using variance analysis and standard costing in a TQM environment?**

☑ For standard costing to be useful for control purposes, it requires a reasonably stable environment.

☑ The ethos behind a system of standard costing is that performance is satisfactory if it meets predetermined standards.

☒ Cost is not important in a TQM environment.

☑ The control aspect of standard costing systems is achieved by making individual managers responsible for the variances relating to their part of the organisation's activities.

☐ Standard costs are set based on ideal standards rather than attainable ones.

1.6 **Which TWO of the following are NOT features of World Class Manufacturing?**

☐ Dedicated cell production
☐ TQM
☑ Absorption costing
☑ Mass production

1.7 **According to one definition of environmental management accounting (EMA), EMA involves identifying, collecting, analysing and using monetary information about environment-related costs and savings, and also:**

☐ Investment returns on environmentally-friendly investment

☑ Physical information about the use and flows of energy, water and materials, including waste and emissions

☐ Impacts on the environment for which the organisation does not incur any direct cost

☐ The profitability of products, allowing for environmental costs

# 2 Environmental costing

2.1 **Which THREE of the following are ways of helping a business to become carbon neutral?**

☐ Encouraging more meetings between employees at different locations to discuss reducing carbon footprint

☐ Reducing energy consumption

☐ Increasing use of renewable electricity

☐ Offsetting

☐ Increasing use of electricity from national grid/country's central supply

2.2 **Using the following list of quality cost classifications, place one of the options next to each one of the costs.**

Classification:

A   Internal failure costs
B   External failure costs
C   Appraisal costs
D   Prevention costs

BPP LEARNING MEDIA

Cost

| | |
|---|---|
| Repairs under warranty | |
| Inspection of goods in | |
| Product design | |
| Lower selling price for sub quality goods | |

2.3 **Which of the following environmental costs would be classified as environmental external failure costs?**

Select ALL that apply.

- ☐ Inspection of product to ensure regulatory compliance
- ☐ Training of employees
- ☑ Cleaning up contaminated soil
- ☑ Government penalties and fines
- ☐ Recycling of waste products

2.4 The following statements have been made about environmental cost accounting:

1 A system of environmental cost accounting provides environmental information for internal use by management, but not for external reporting.

2 Environmental management accounting systems typically make use of life cycle costing.

**Which of the above statements is/are true?**

- ☑ 1 only
- ☐ 2 only
- ☐ Neither 1 nor 2
- ☑ Both 1 and 2

# 3a Absorption costing

3a.1 DEF Co publishes three newspapers, The Post, The Gazette and The News. The following information has been obtained from the accounting system for period 6:

| | The Post | The Gazette | The News |
|---|---|---|---|
| Number published | 60,000 | 80,000 | 90,000 |
| Direct labour hours per unit | 0.2 | 0.3 | 0.1 |
| Machine hours per unit | 0.4 | 0.5 | 0.3 |
| Set-ups | 4 | 3 | 3 |
| Distribution outlets | 15 | 18 | 12 |

Overheads are related to the following activities:

| Activities | Cost of activities |
|---|---|
| | $ |
| Distribution | 22,500 |
| Machine maintenance | 24,570 |
| Machine set-up | 25,730 |
| | 72,800 |

**What is the traditional overhead absorption rate for period 6? (give your answer to 2 dp)**

$ [          ]

**3a.2** **Overheads will always be over-absorbed in which of these circumstances:**

- ☐ Actual output is higher than budgeted output.
- ☐ Actual overheads incurred are higher than the amount absorbed.
- ☑ Actual overheads incurred are lower than the amount absorbed.
- ☐ Budgeted overheads are lower than the overheads absorbed.

---

**3a.3** **Which of the following statements about predetermined overhead absorption rates are true?**

(i) Using a predetermined absorption rate avoids fluctuations in unit costs caused by abnormally high or low overhead expenditure or activity levels.

(ii) Using a predetermined absorption rate offers the administrative convenience of being able to record full production costs sooner.

(iii) Using a predetermined absorption rate avoids problems of under/over absorption of overheads because a constant overhead rate is available.

- ☑ (i) and (ii) only
- ☐ (i) and (iii) only
- ☐ (ii) and (iii) only
- ☐ All of them

---

**3a.4** A company has over-absorbed fixed production overheads for the period by $6,000. The fixed production overhead absorption rate was $8 per unit and is based on the normal level of activity of 5,000 units. Actual production was 4,500 units.

**What were the actual fixed production overheads incurred for the period?**

- ☐ $30,000
- ☐ $36,000
- ☐ $40,000
- ☐ $42,000

---

**3a.5** RJD Co operates a standard absorption costing system. The following fixed production overhead data is available for one month:

| | |
|---|---|
| Budgeted output | 200,000 units |
| Budgeted fixed production overhead | $1,000,000 |
| Actual fixed production overhead | $1,300,000 |
| Total fixed production overhead variance | $100,000 Adverse |

**The actual level of production was:**

- ☐ 180,000 units
- ☑ 240,000 units
- ☐ 270,000 units
- ☐ 280,000 units

BPP LEARNING MEDIA

3a.6 A company operates a standard absorption costing system and absorbs fixed production overheads based on machine hours. The budgeted fixed production overheads for the company for the previous year were $660,000 and budgeted output was 220,000 units using 44,000 machine hours. During that year, the total of the fixed production overheads debited to the Fixed Production Overhead Control Account was $590,000, and the actual output of 200,000 units used 38,000 machine hours.

**Fixed production overheads for that year were:**

☐ $90,000 under absorbed.
☐ $60,000 under absorbed.
☐ $20,000 under absorbed.
☑ $10,000 over absorbed.

---

3a.7 A company produces and sells one type of product. The details for last year were as follows:

Production and sales

|  | *Budget* | *Actual* |
|---|---|---|
| Production (units) | 25,000 | 22,000 |
| Sales (units) | 23,000 | 20,000 |

There was no inventory at the start of the year.

Selling price and costs

|  | *Budget* | *Actual* |
|---|---|---|
|  | $ | $ |
| Selling price per unit | 70 | 70 |
| Variable costs per unit | 55 | 55 |
| Fixed production overhead | 130,000 | 118,000 |
| Fixed selling costs | 75,000 | 75,000 |

**Calculate the actual profit for the year that would be reported using absorption costing.**

$ 11,740

---

3a.8 **Over-absorbed overheads occur when:**

☐ Absorbed overheads exceed budgeted overheads.
☐ Actual overheads exceed absorbed overheads.
☐ Actual overheads exceed budgeted overheads.
☑ Absorbed overheads exceed actual overheads.

---

3a.9 A company produced 5,000 units of Product B last month. The opening and closing inventory of Product B was 400 units and 900 units respectively. The selling price and production costs for Product B were as follows:

|  | $ per unit |
|---|---|
| Selling price | 20.00 |
| Direct costs | 6.00 |
| Variable production overhead costs | 3.50 |
| Fixed production overhead costs | 5.90 |
| Gross profit | 4.60 |

**What is the gross profit for Product B last month, using absorption costing?**

(Give your answer to the nearest whole $)

$

3a.10  A company uses a standard absorption costing system. The fixed overhead absorption rate is based on labour hours.

Extracts from the company's records for the last year were as follows:

|  | Budget | Actual |
|---|---|---|
| Fixed production overhead | $540,000 | $570,000 |
| Output | 60,000 units | 72,000 units |
| Labour hours | 1,080,000 | 1,110,000 |

**The under or over absorbed fixed production overheads for the year were:**

- ☐ $15,000 under absorbed
- ☐ $15,000 over absorbed
- ☐ $30,000 over absorbed
- ☐ $78,000 over absorbed

# 3b Activity based costing

3b.1  **Which of the following is NOT used as the basis for absorbing production overheads in a traditional absorption costing system?**

- ☑ Number of production runs
- ☐ Number of machine hours
- ☐ Number of labour hours
- ☑ Number of set ups

3b.2  A company has total overheads of $735,000 of which $488,000 relates to machine use, $85,000 to production set-ups and the balance to handling of orders.

The company has two products X and Y, and expects the following in the next period.

|  | X | Y |
|---|---|---|
| Quantity made | 12,000 | 25,000 |
| Direct labour hours per unit | 2 | 1 |
| Machine hours per unit | 3 | 1 |
| Total number of production set-ups | 10 | 40 |
| Total number of orders | 16 | 20 |

Calculate the overheads absorbed by each unit of X using an ABC approach and suitable cost drivers.

Give your answer to 2dp.

**The overheads absorbed by each unit of X are: $** ☐

3b.3  The following statements relate to activity based costing:

(i)   Activity-based costs can be used to identify relevant costs for short-term decision making.
(ii)  Activity-based costing cannot be used to cost services.
(iii) Activity-based costing is a form of absorption costing.
(iv)  Activity-based costing is an alternative to traditional volume-based costing methods.

**Which statements are true?**

- ☐ (i) only
- ☐ (ii) only
- ☑ (ii) and (iii)
- ☑ (iii) and (iv)

BPP
LEARNING MEDIA

3b.4 A single-product company has the following results for its financial year:

| | $'000 |
|---|---|
| Sales | 13,000 |
| Direct material costs | (2,600) |
| Direct labour costs | (1,300) |
| Fixed overheads | (1,000) |
| Net profit | 8,100 |

Production for the year was 130,000 units.

The company has performed an activity-based costing exercise and has traced its overheads to the following cost pools:

| Cost pool | % of total overhead | Cost driver | Activity level |
|---|---|---|---|
| Order processing | 25 | Orders processed | 50,000 |
| Sales force salaries | 40 | Sales force hours worked | 20,000 |
| Research | 35 | Department hours worked | 10,000 |

Customer X made 400 orders during the year, required 300 hours of sales force time, 100 hours of research and purchased 1,000 units during the year.

**Calculate the profit attributable to customer X under activity-based costing:**

- ☐ $58,500
- ☐ $60,000
- ☐ $62,308
- ☐ $81,000

---

3b.5 **Which of the following statements about activity based costing is/are correct?**

(I) Short-term variable overhead costs should be traced to products using volume-related cost drivers, such as machine hours or direct labour hours.

(II) Long-term variable production overhead costs are driven partly by the complexity and diversity of production work, as well as by the volume of output.

(III) Transactions undertaken by support department personnel are the appropriate cost drivers for long-term variable overhead costs.

(IV) Overheads should be charged to products on the basis of their usage of an activity. A product's usage of an activity is measured by the number of the activity's cost driver it generates.

- ☐ All of the above
- ☐ I only
- ☐ II only
- ☑ I, III and IV

---

3b.6 The following data relates to production of A Co's three products in period 6.

| | Product X | Product Y | Product Z |
|---|---|---|---|
| Production and sales (units) | 300 | 200 | 150 |
| Machine hours per unit | 30 | 10 | 10 |
| No of production runs | 7 | 2 | 1 |
| No of deliveries to customers | 5 | 5 | 5 |
| No of deliveries of material into store | 20 | 19 | 1 |

| | $ |
|---|---|
| Machining | 35,750 |
| Set-up costs | 5,250 |
| Materials handling (receiving) | 17,500 |
| Packing costs (despatch) | 22,500 |

**What is the overhead cost per unit of product Y using activity based costing?**

- ☐ $150.55
- ☐ $112.91
- ☐ $525
- ☐ $2.86

---

**3b.7** Activity based costing (ABC) is claimed to provide more accurate product costs than a traditional absorption costing system.

**Which of the following statements does NOT support this claim?**

- ☐ ABC uses cost drivers to allocate overhead costs to products by cost pool ╱
- ☒ ABC identifies value added and non-value added activities
- ☐ ABC assigns overheads to each major activity
- ☐ ABC uses both volume based and non-volume based cost drivers

---

**3b.8** A company uses an activity based costing system. Three products are manufactured, details of which are given below:

|  | Product A | Product B | Product C |
|---|---|---|---|
| Annual production (units) | 80,000 | 100,000 | 50,000 |
| Batch size (units) | 100 | 50 | 25 |
| Machine set-ups per batch | 3 | 4 | 6 |

Annual machine set-up costs are $150,000.

**The machine set-up cost per unit of Product B (to the nearest $0.01) is:**

- ☐ $0.46
- ☐ $0.65
- ☐ $6.70
- ☐ $0.54

---

**3b.9** A company uses an activity based costing system to attribute overhead costs to its three products. The following budget data relates to this year:

| Product | X | Y | Z |
|---|---|---|---|
| Production (units) | 50,000 | 25,000 | 20,000 |
| Batch size | 250 | 100 | 400 |

Material handling costs are determined by the number of batches of each product and have been estimated to be $60,000 for the year.

**What is the cost driver rate for material handling costs?**

Give your answer to the nearest whole $

$ [        ]

---

**3b.10 Classify the following activity based costs incurred in a multi product manufacturing environment by placing the activities next to the costs below:**

A    Batch level activities
B    Product sustaining activities
C    Facility sustaining activities
D    Unit level activities

BPP LEARNING MEDIA

Purchase order processing costs ▢

Product advertising costs ▢

Factory rent and rates ▢

Direct labour costs ▢

Product redesign costs ▢

Material handling costs ▢

3b.11 Happy plc makes two products Smile and Tickle. The following information has been given to you:

| | Smile | Tickle |
|---|---|---|
| Production (units) | 400 | 1,600 |
| Machine hrs/unit | 6 | 8 |
| Production runs | 5 | 2 |
| Inspections (during production) | 3 | 6 |

| | |
|---|---|
| Production set up costs | $134,400 |
| Quality control costs | $55,200 |

**Using activity based costing, calculate which ONE of the following is the overhead cost per unit of product Tickle:**

▢ $57.20
☑ $47.00
▢ $71.50
▢ $286.00

# 4 Marginal costing and throughput accounting

4.1 The following details have been extracted from the budget papers of LK plc for June 20X3.

| | |
|---|---|
| Selling price per unit | $124 |
| Variable production costs per unit | $54 |
| Fixed production costs per unit | $36 |
| Other variable costs per unit | $12 |
| Sales volume | 12,500 units |
| Production volume | 13,250 units |
| Opening inventory of finished items | 980 units |

**If budgeted profit statements were prepared by using absorption costing and then by using marginal costing:**

▢ marginal costing profits would be higher by $27,000
☑ absorption costing profits would be higher by $27,000
▢ absorption costing profits would be higher by $35,000
▢ absorption costing profits would be higher by $62,000

**4.2** A company produces and sells one type of product. The details for last year were as follows:

Production and sales

| | Budget | Actual |
|---|---|---|
| Production (units) | 25,000 | 22,000 |
| Sales (units) | 23,000 | 20,000 |

There was no inventory at the start of the year.

Selling price and costs

| | Budget $ | Actual $ |
|---|---|---|
| Selling price per unit | 70 | 70 |
| Variable costs per unit | 55 | 55 |
| Fixed production overhead | 130,000 | 118,000 |
| Fixed selling costs | 75,000 | 75,000 |

**Calculate the actual profit for the year that would be reported using marginal costing.**

$ [_____] ('000)

---

**4.3** **Which of the following features distinguish throughput accounting from other costing systems?**

- ☐ Work in progress is valued at labour cost only.
- ☐ Work in progress is valued at material cost only.
- ☐ Costs are allocated to products when they are completed or sold.
- ☐ Only labour cost is treated as a variable cost.

---

**4.4** A company produces three products using three different machines. No other products are made on these particular machines. The following data is available for December 20X3:

| | A | B | C |
|---|---|---|---|
| Contribution per unit | $36 | $28 | $18 |
| Machine hours required per unit: | | | |
| Machine 1 | 5 | 2 | 1.5 |
| Machine 2 | 5 | 5.5 | 1.5 |
| Machine 3 | 2.5 | 1 | 0.5 |
| Estimated sales demand (units) | 50 | 50 | 60 |

Maximum machine capacity in December will be 400 hours per machine.

**Calculate the machine utilisation rates for each machine for December 20X3 and identify which is the bottleneck machine(s).**

- ☐ Machine 1
- ☐ Machine 2
- ☐ Machine 3
- ☐ Machines 1 and 2
- ☐ Machines 1 and 3

---

**4.5** **Which of these explanations of shadow prices is/are correct?**

1 The additional contribution generated from one additional unit of limiting factor.
2 The opportunity cost of not having the use of one extra unit of limiting factor.
3 The maximum amount that should be paid for one additional unit of scarce resource.

- ☐ 2 and 3
- ☐ 1 and 2
- ☐ 1 and 3
- ☐ All statements are correct

BPP LEARNING MEDIA

4.6 PQ Co produces a single product. The budgeted fixed production overheads for the period are $400,000. The budgeted output for the period is 2,000 units. Opening inventory at the start of the period consisted of 1,800 units and closing inventory at the end of the period consisted of 900 units.

**If absorption costing principles were applied, the profit for the period compared to the marginal costing profit would be:**

- ☐ $540,000 higher
- ☐ $540,000 lower
- ☐ $180,000 higher
- ☐ $180,000 lower

---

4.7 JH Co produces three products, the L1, the L2 and the L3. The L1 has a TA ratio of 1.4, the L2 a ratio of 1.8, and the L3 has a ratio of 1.0.

**Which of the following statements is/are true?**

- ☐ L1 should be produced before L2.
- ☐ L3 should be produced before L1.
- ☐ L3 should not be produced at all.
- ☐ Only L3 should be produced.
- ☐ It is impossible to state a preference between the products.
- ☐ None of the above statements are true.

---

4.8 **When comparing the profits reported under absorption costing and marginal costing during a period when the level of inventory increased:**

- ☐ Absorption costing profits will be higher and closing inventory valuations lower than those under marginal costing

- ☐ Absorption costing profits will be higher and closing inventory valuations higher than those under marginal costing

- ☐ Marginal costing profits will be higher and closing inventory valuations lower than those under absorption costing

- ☐ Marginal costing profits will be higher and closing inventory valuations higher than those under absorption costing

---

4.9 J provides three different payroll services to businesses that cannot justify operating their own payroll departments. The following contribution and sales values have been determined for each of these services:

| Service | X | Y | Z |
|---|---|---|---|
| Sales value per service ($) | 100 | 200 | 100 |
| Contribution per service ($) | 40 | 70 | 25 |

**If equal quantities of X, Y and Z are to be sold and fixed costs are $100,000 per month, the monthly sales value that would result in a profit of $40,000 is nearest to:**

- ☐ $311,000
- ☐ $336,000
- ☐ $415,000
- ☐ $420,000

4.10 The following statements have been made about pricing:

(i) The mark up used in marginal costing is less arbitrary than the mark up used in full cost pricing.

(ii) The level of competition in the market is ignored under both full cost and marginal cost plus pricing.

(iii) The price elasticity of demand can be used to assess the impact on total revenue of changing the selling price of a product.

**Which of the above statements are true?**

☐ (i) and (ii)
☐ (ii) and (iii)
☐ (i) and (iii)
☐ (i), (ii) and (iii)

4.11 The following statements have been made about pricing:

(i) When calculating a mark-up and a margin on the same product, the margin will be a higher percentage than the mark-up

(ii) Using full cost pricing ensures that a product will generate a profit for the business

(iii) Marginal cost plus pricing is a form of relevant costing

**Which of the above statements are true?**

☐ (i) and (ii)
☐ (ii) and (iii)
☐ (i) and (iii)
☐ None of them

# 5 Limiting factor analysis

5.1 Z Co manufactures three products, the selling price and cost details of which are given below:

|  | Product X | Product Y | Product Z |
|---|---|---|---|
|  | $ | $ | $ |
| Selling price per unit | 75 | 95 | 96 |
| Costs per unit: |  |  |  |
| Direct materials ($5/kg) | 10 | 5 | 15 |
| Direct labour ($4/hour) | 16 | 24 | 20 |
| Variable overhead | 8 | 12 | 10 |
| Fixed overhead | 24 | 36 | 30 |

**In a period when direct materials are restricted in supply, the most and the least profitable uses of direct materials are:**

|  | Most profitable | Least profitable |
|---|---|---|
| A | Y | X |
| B | Y | Z |
| C | Z | X |
| D | Z | Y |

BPP LEARNING MEDIA

5.2 MNP plc produces three products from a single raw material that is limited in supply. Product details for period 6 are as follows:

|  | Product M | Product N | Product P |
|---|---|---|---|
| Maximum demand (units) | 1,000 | 2,400 | 2,800 |
| Optimum planned production | 720 | nil | 2,800 |
| Unit contribution | $4.50 | $4.80 | $2.95 |
| Raw material cost per unit ($0.50 per kg) | $1.25 | $1.50 | $0.75 |

The planned production optimises the use of the 6,000 kgs of raw material that is available from MNP plc's normal supplier at the price of $0.50 kg. However, a new supplier has been found that is prepared to supply a further 1,000 kgs of the material.

**Calculate the maximum price that MNP plc should be prepared to pay for the additional 1,000 kgs of the material.**

$ [            ]

---

5.3 **Which THREE of the following statements regarding marginal and absorption costing are true in the context of pricing decisions?**

- ☐ Marginal costing is appropriate for long-term pricing decisions.
- ☐ Marginal costing is appropriate for short-term pricing decisions.
- ☐ Absorption costing when used for pricing decisions includes the 'total-cost' of the product.
- ☐ Marginal costing ensures the recovery of all costs incurred in selling prices.
- ☐ Marginal costing is more appropriate than absorption costing for use in one-off pricing decisions.
- ☐ Absorption costing is more appropriate than marginal costing for use in one-off pricing decisions.

---

5.4 A company manufactures three products D, E and F. The company currently has a shortage of skilled labour, with total hours restricted to 5,400.

Details of these products are:

|  | D | E | F |
|---|---|---|---|
| Demand (units) | 2,400 | 2,200 | 3,000 |
| Contribution per unit | 54 | 72 | 35 |
| Skilled labour hours per unit | 1 | 1.5 | 0.5 |

**The mix of products that will maximise contribution is:**

- ☐ (2,200 × E) + (2,100 × D)
- ☐ (1,000 × E) + (2,400 × D) + (3,000 × F)
- ☐ (2,200 × E) + (600 × D) + (3,000 × F)
- ☐ (2,400 × D) + (2,200 × E) + (3,000 × F)

---

5.5 The following data relates to Product W.

|  | Per unit |
|---|---|
| Selling price | $26.00 |
| Material cost | $7.25 |
| Labour cost | $5.75 |
| Overhead cost | $5.00 |
| Time on bottleneck resource | 7 minutes |

**Using throughput accounting, the contribution per hour for Product W is:**

- ☐ $68.57
- ☐ $106.75
- ☐ $130.71
- ☐ $160.71

5.6    A manufacturing company recorded the following costs in October for Product X:

|  | $ |
|---|---|
| Direct materials | 20,000 |
| Direct labour | 6,300 |
| Variable production overhead | 4,700 |
| Fixed production overhead | 19,750 |
| Variable selling costs | 4,500 |
| Fixed distribution costs | 16,800 |
| Total costs incurred for Product X | 72,050 |

During October 4,000 units of Product X were produced but only 3,600 units were sold. At the beginning of October there was no inventory.

**The value of the inventory of Product X at the end of October using throughput accounting was:**

☐    $630
☐    $1,080
☐    $1,100
☐    $2,000

---

5.7    In a time when labour supply is limited, a company has identified that it has 400 hours of labour available and that there is unlimited demand for each of its three products. Labour is paid $5 per hour.

|  | A | B | C |
|---|---|---|---|
|  | $ | $ | $ |
| Sales price per unit | 20 | 23 | 25 |
| Material cost per unit | 3 | 2 | 4 |
| Labour cost per unit | 5 | 10 | 7.5 |

**What is the optimal production plan?**

☐    Produce 400 As
☐    Produce 200 Bs
☐    Produce 200 Cs
☐    Produce 200 As, 100 Bs and 200 Cs

---

5.8    Z plc manufactures three products which have the following selling prices and costs per unit:

|  | Z1 | Z2 | Z3 |
|---|---|---|---|
|  | $ | $ | $ |
| Selling price | 15.00 | 18.00 | 17.00 |
| Costs per unit: |  |  |  |
| Direct materials | 4.00 | 5.00 | 10.00 |
| Direct labour | 2.00 | 4.00 | 1.80 |
| Overhead: |  |  |  |
| Variable | 1.00 | 2.00 | 0.90 |
| Fixed | 4.50 | 3.00 | 1.35 |
|  | 11.50 | 14.00 | 14.05 |
| Profit per unit | 3.50 | 4.00 | 2.95 |

All three products use the same type of labour.

**In a period in which labour is in short supply, the rank order of production is:**

|  | Z1 | Z2 | Z3 |
|---|---|---|---|
| A | First | Second | Third |
| B | Third | Second | First |
| C | Second | First | Third |
| D | First | Third | Second |

5.9 JR Co's accountant has correctly identified the scarce resource for the period is direct labour. He has calculated that the shadow price of direct labour is $4.50 per hour. Direct labour is currently paid $10 per hour.

**If the objective of the company is to maximise profit in each period, how much should the company be willing to pay per hour to obtain additional direct labour hours of production capacity?**

- ☐ Up to but not including $4.50
- ☐ Up to and including $4.50
- ☐ Up to but not including $14.50
- ☐ Up to and including $14.50

5.10 **Which of these actions are recommended in the procedure given by Goldratt in his 'Theory of Constraints' for dealing with a bottleneck activity?**

- ☐ Buffer stock at each stage of production
- ☐ Subordinate operations to binding constraint
- ☐ Identify binding constraint
- ☐ Reward improved performance
- ☐ Exploit the available capacity

# 6 Relevant costs

6.1 S Co is considering adapting its assembly process so that products can also be moulded at the same time. The existing assembly process machinery would have to be removed, either now at a dismantling cost of $100,000 and with the sale of the machinery for $800,000, or in one year's time at a dismantling cost of $110,000 and with sale proceeds of $600,000. Alternative machinery would have to be leased. This would cost $80,000 per annum. The existing assembly process machinery originally cost $2,000,000 when purchased seven years ago. It is being depreciated at 5% per annum on a straight line basis.

**Analysing on an incremental opportunity cost basis and ignoring the time value of money, which of the following is correct?**

- ☐ Adapting now will produce savings of $130,000 more than adapting in one year.
- ☐ Adapting now will cost $130,000 more than adapting in one year.
- ☐ Adapting now will produce savings of $110,000 more than adapting in one year.
- ☐ Adapting now will cost $110,000 more than adapting in one year.

6.2 D Co's entire machine capacity is used to produce essential components. The variable costs of using the machines are $150,000 and the fixed costs are $400,000. If all the components were purchased from an outside supplier, the machines could be used to produce other items which would earn a total contribution of $250,000.

**The maximum price that D Co should be willing to pay to the outside supplier for the components, assuming there is no change in fixed costs is:**

$ _____

**6.3**    A special job for a customer will required 8 tonnes of a Material M. The company no longer uses this material regularly although it holds 3 tonnes in inventory. These originally cost $44 per tonne, and could be resold to a supplier for $35 per tonne. Alternatively these materials could be used to complete another job instead of using other materials that would cost $126 in total to purchase. The current market price of Material M is $50 per tonne. The company must decide whether to agree to the customer's request for the work, and to set a price.

**What would be the relevant cost of Material M for this job?**

☐    $250
☐    $355
☐    $376
☐    $400

---

**6.4**    **Which of the following are non-relevant costs?**

Select ALL that apply.

☐    Avoidable costs
☐    Opportunity costs
☐    Notional costs
☐    Sunk costs

---

**6.5**    A company is considering the use of material X in a special order. A sufficient quantity of the material, which is used regularly by the company in its normal business is available from inventory.

**What is the relevant cost per kg of material X in the evaluation of the special order?**

☐    Cost of the last purchase
☐    Nil
☐    Replacement cost
☐    Saleable value

---

**6.6**    Sherburn plc has sufficient material Y in inventory for a year's production of 'stringfree'. Material Y cost $8,000 but is subject to major price variations; the current market price is double the original cost. It could be sold at the market price less 15% selling expenses. An alternative is to retain it for later use by which time the market price is expected to be $11,200.

**The relevant cost of using material Y on the contract is:**

$ [                    ]

---

**6.7**    The following information is available for identifying the relevant cost of materials for a job for a customer. The company's management wants to establish a minimum price at which it is prepared to take on the job.

| Material | Total quantity required | Currently in inventory | Carrying value per kg | Realisable value per kg | Replacement cost per kg |
|---|---|---|---|---|---|
|  | kg | kg | $ | $ | $ |
| X | 500 | 300 | 5 | 3 | 7 |
| Y | 500 | 400 | 8 | 9 | 11 |
| Z | 100 | 100 | 10 | 12 | 15 |

Material Y is in regular use by the company. Materials X and Z are no longer in regular use.

**What is the relevant cost of these materials for the job under consideration?**

☐    $9,000
☐    $6,000
☐    $7,600
☐    $9,300

---

BPP
LEARNING MEDIA

6.8 What is the relevant cost of units of finished goods when disposing of them if they are no longer required?

- ☐ Net realisable value
- ☐ Replacement cost
- ☐ Variable cost
- ☐ Full cost

6.9 When analysing whether to replace an asset, which ONE of the following is not relevant?

- ☐ Balancing charge or allowance on the old asset
- ☐ Book value of the old asset
- ☐ Changes in working capital
- ☐ Removal costs of the old asset

6.10 X Co has 500kg of material K in inventory for which it paid $2,000. The material is no longer in use in the company and could be sold for $1.50 per kg.

X Co is considering taking on a special order which will require 800kg of material K. The current purchase price is $5 per kg.

In the assessment of the relevant cost of the decision to accept the special order, the cost of material K is:

- ☐ A sunk cost of $2,000
- ☐ A sunk cost of $2,000 and an incremental cost of $1,500
- ☐ An opportunity cost of $750 and an incremental cost of $1,500
- ☐ An incremental cost of $4,000.

# 7 Multi-product breakeven analysis

7.1 Which two out of the following four options show how the breakeven point in units can be calculated?

- ☐ Total fixed costs/contribution per unit
- ☐ Contribution required to break even/contribution per unit
- ☐ Contribution/sales
- ☐ Fixed costs/costs to sales ratio

7.2 The following information is available for S Co.

|  | $'000 |
|---|---|
| Revenue | 1,000 |
| Variable costs | 600 |
| Fixed costs | 250 |
| Profit | 150 |

Assuming that the sales mix does not change, what increase in sales revenue would need to be achieved to increase the profit to $250,000?

- ☐ $150,000
- ☐ $400,000
- ☐ $100,000
- ☐ $250,000

**7.3** A company provides three different levels of customer service support for one of its software products.

The following data relate to these three levels of support:

| Support level | Superior<br>$ per contract | Standard<br>$ per contract | Basic<br>$ per contract |
|---|---|---|---|
| Annual fee | 1,000 | 750 | 400 |
| Annual variable costs | 450 | 250 | 180 |
| Annual fixed costs (see note below) | 200 | 100 | 50 |
| Profit | 350 | 400 | 170 |

Note: The total annual fixed costs are budgeted to be $1,000,000. None of these costs are specific to any type of customer service support.

Assume that the number of customer service support contracts sold are in the proportion:

Superior 20%         Standard 30%         Basic 50%

**What is the annual revenue needed to break even?**

(Give your answer to the nearest thousand)

$ [           ]

---

**7.4** A company makes and sells three products, R, S, and T. Extracts from the weekly profit statements are as follows.

| | R<br>$ | S<br>$ | T<br>$ | Total<br>$ |
|---|---|---|---|---|
| Sales | 10,000 | 15,000 | 20,000 | 45,000 |
| Variable cost of sales | 4,000 | 9,000 | 10,000 | 23,000 |
| Fixed costs* | 3,000 | 3,000 | 3,000 | 9,000 |
| Profit | 3,000 | 3,000 | 7,000 | 13,000 |

*general fixed costs absorbed using a unit absorption rate

**If the sales revenue mix of products produced and sold were to be changed to: R 20%, S 50%, T 30% then the new average contribution to sales ratio would be:**

☐    Higher
☐    Lower
☐    Unchanged

---

**7.5** A company sells three different levels of TV maintenance contract to its customers: Basic, Standard and Advanced. Selling prices, unit costs and monthly sales are as follows:

| | Basic<br>$ | Standard<br>$ | Advanced<br>$ |
|---|---|---|---|
| Selling price | 50 | 100 | 135 |
| Variable cost | 30 | 50 | 65 |
| Monthly contracts sold | 750 | 450 | 300 |

**The average contribution to sales ratio of the company based on this sales mix is:**

[           ] %

---

**7.6** F Scuttle Co has fixed costs of $50,000 per annum.

The company sells a single product for $25 per unit.

The contribution to sales ratio is 40%.

**What is the breakeven point in revenue?**

Breakeven point at $ [           ]

BPP
LEARNING MEDIA

7.7 Blob Co has a budgeted breakeven sales revenue of $2 million and fixed costs of $800,000 for the month of June. The directors of Blob Co want to make a profit of $125,000.

**What is the sales revenue that Blob Co needs to achieve?**

- ☐ $2,800,000
- ☐ $3,000,000
- ☐ $2,312,500
- ☐ $2,125,000

---

7.8 A company provides a number of different services to its customers from a single office. The fixed costs of the office, including staff costs, are absorbed into the company's service costs using an absorption rate of $25 per consulting hour based on a budgeted activity level of 25,000 each quarter.

**Fee income and variable costs are different depending on the services provided, but the average contribution to sales ratio is 35%. The breakeven annual fee income is closest to:**

- ☐ $1,786,000
- ☐ $219,000
- ☐ $875,000
- ☐ $7,143,000

---

7.9 RDF Co offers four services to television companies The number of services provided is measured in service units and details of RDF Co's draft budget for its year ending 30 June 20X5 are as follows.

|  | Service K | Service L | Service M | Service N |
|---|---|---|---|---|
| Number of service units | 1,000 | 2,300 | 1,450 | 1,970 |
| Selling price per unit ($) | 18 | 16 | 12 | 20 |
| Variable cost per unit ($) | 8 | 10 | 13 | 13 |
| Fixed cost per unit ($) | 2 | 3 | 2 | 4 |

The budgeted level of activity shown in the table above has been based on fully meeting the forecasted market demand for each type of service.

The following chart has been prepared based on the draft budget above.

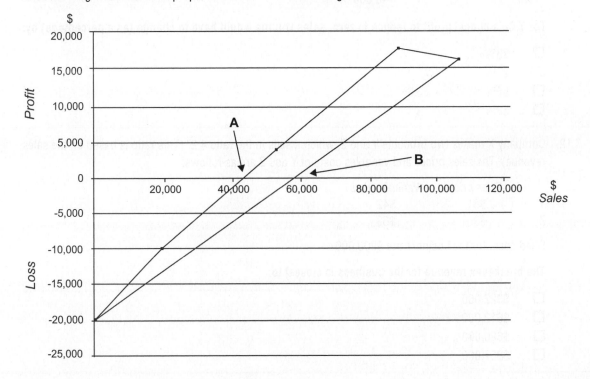

Choose options from the list below to correctly label points A and B of the multi product profit volume graph.

- Multi product break even point
- Break even point if services sold in the order K L N M
- Break even point if services sold in the order K M L N
- Break even point if services sold in the order L K M N

Point A: [            ]

Point B: [            ]

---

7.10 PER plc sells three products. The budgeted fixed cost for the period is $648,000. The budgeted contribution to sales ratio (C/S ratio) and sales mix are as follows

| Product | C/S ratio | Mix |
|---------|-----------|-----|
| P | 27% | 30% |
| E | 56% | 20% |
| R | 38% | 50% |

**The breakeven revenue is:**

Give your answer in '000 to the nearest whole thousand.

$ [            ]

---

7.11 T Co has prepared its budget for the next year, aiming to produce and sell 600,000 units. The following forecasts have also been made:

|  | $ |
|--|---|
| Sales | 500,000 |
| Material costs | (90,000) |
| Labour costs | (80,000) |
| Variable overheads | (30,000) |
| Fixed overheads | (160,000) |
| Profit | 140,000 |

**For T Co's budget profit to reduce to zero, sales volume would have to change (as a percentage) by:**

- ☐ 23%
- ☐ 27%
- ☐ 50%
- ☐ 53%

---

7.12 Company X makes two products Y and Z, which it sells in the ratio 4:2. (This ratio is based on the sales revenue). The sales prices and variables costs of Y and Z are as follows:

|  | Sales price | Variable costs |
|--|-------------|----------------|
| Y | $61 | $42 |
| Z | $95 | $63 |

Fixed costs for the business are $200,000.

**The breakeven revenue for the business is closest to:**

- ☐ $322,000
- ☐ $612,000
- ☐ $620,000
- ☐ $857,000

BPP LEARNING MEDIA

7.13 A company makes two different products in two different departments. Each department makes only one product.

Product A has a contribution to sales ratio of 0.7
Product B has a contribution to sales ratio of 0.74
Both are selling above their breakeven points

**Based on the information provided which of the following statements is true?**

☐ Variable costs in product A are 4% higher than in product B

☐ Product B will have a lower break-even point than product A

☐ The contribution earned by Product B grows more quickly than the contribution earned by product A as sales levels increase

☐ 70% of the selling price of product B contributes to fixed overheads and profits

# 8 Short term decision making

8.1 L Co operates a process which produces three joint products: M, N and P. The costs of operating this process during control period 4 totalled $210,600. During the period the output of the three products was:

| | |
|---|---|
| M | 3,600 kgs |
| N | 8,100 kgs |
| P | 5,850 kgs |

N is further processed at a cost of $16.20 per kg. The actual loss in the second process was 10% of input, which is normal. Products M and P are sold without further processing.

The final selling prices of each product are:

| | |
|---|---|
| M | $36 per kg |
| N | $32.40 per kg |
| P | $45 per kg |

**Calculate the profit for Product N.**

$ [          ]

8.2 **If a company has to subcontract work to make up a shortfall in its own in-house capabilities, how will its total costs be minimised?**

☐ If those units bought from the subcontractor are the cheapest to buy.

☐ If those units bought from the subcontractor have the lowest extra variable cost per unit of scarce resource saved.

☐ If those units bought from the subcontractor have the highest extra variable cost per unit of scarce resource saved.

☐ If those units produced in house are the most expensive to produce.

8.3 **Which of the following is NOT a valid reason why the costs used for decision making may be different from the costs used for profit reporting?**

☐ Costs used for decision making include only costs that are affected by the decision
☐ Costs used for decision making never include fixed costs
☐ Costs used for decision making do not include past costs
☐ Costs used for decision making include opportunity costs

8.4    The performance of the three divisions of a company is detailed below:

|  | Division W | Division X | Division Y | Total |
|---|---|---|---|---|
|  | $'000 | $'000 | $'000 | $'000 |
| Sales | 700 | 840 | 300 | 1,840 |
| Variable costs | 560 | 420 | 240 | 1,220 |
| Contribution | 140 | 420 | 60 | 620 |
| Fixed overheads |  |  |  | 525 |
| Net profit |  |  |  | 95 |

40% of the fixed overheads are specific to the individual divisions. Each division incurs the same level of specific fixed overheads.

**Which of the divisions should continue to operate if the company's objective is to maximise profits?**

☐    All of divisions
☐    Division W and Division X only
☐    Division X only
☐    Division X and Division Y only

---

8.5    **Which of the following is an example of a feedback control?**

☐    Variance analysis
☐    Cash flow forecasting
☐    Forecasting future prices
☐    Budget setting process

---

8.6    A company simultaneously produces three products (X, Y and Z) from a single process. X and Y are processed further before they can be sold.  Z is a by-product that is sold immediately for $6 per unit without incurring any further costs. The sales prices of X and Y after further processing are $50 per unit and $60 per unit respectively. Data for October are as follows:

|  | $ |
|---|---|
| Joint production costs that produced 2,500 units of X, 3,500 units of Y and 3,000 units of Z | 140,000 |
| Further processing costs for 2,500 units of X | 24,000 |
| Further processing costs for 3,500 units of Y | 46,000 |

Joint costs are apportioned using the final sales value method.

**Calculate the total cost of the production of X for October.**

$ ⬚

---

8.7    HM Co has to decide whether to make component B in-house or to buy it from an external supplier. The costs to make component B are as follows:

|  | $ |
|---|---|
| Variable cost | 35,000 |
| Fixed cost | 50,000 |
|  | 85,000 |

If component B is purchased from a supplier then other items could be produced instead which would earn a total contribution of $45,000

**Calculate the maximum price that HM Co would be willing to pay to the supplier for component B.**

$ ⬚

BPP
LEARNING MEDIA

8.8    A company is preparing a quotation for a one-off job that would require 1,200kg of Material B. There are 900kg of Material B in inventory that were bought at a cost of $3 per kg. The company does not foresee any other use for the material. The material held in inventory could be sold for $3.50 per kg. The current purchase price of Material B is $4.50 per kg.

**The relevant cost of Material B to be included in the cost estimate is:**

☐    $4,050
☐    $4,500
☐    $4,200
☐    $5,400

8.9    **A company makes three components, X, Y and Z. The costs to manufacture the components are as follows:**

|  | X | Y | Z |
|---|---|---|---|
|  | $ | $ | $ |
| Variable cost | 5.00 | 16.00 | 10.00 |
| Fixed cost | 4.00 | 16.60 | 7.50 |
| Total unit cost | 9.00 | 32.60 | 17.50 |

The fixed costs are an allocation of general fixed overheads.

A supplier has offered to supply the components at the following prices:

Component X    $8
Component Y    $14
Component Z    $11

**Which components should the company buy in order to minimise total costs?**

☐    Components X and Z
☐    Component Y only
☐    None of the components
☐    All of the components

8.10   **Which THREE of the following are categories of relevant costs?**

☐    Incremental costs
☐    Committed costs
☐    Sunk costs
☐    Differential costs
☐    Absorbed fixed costs
☐    Opportunity costs

8.11   ABC Co makes three products, budget information is provided below.

|  | A | B | C |
|---|---|---|---|
|  | $ | $ | $ |
| Selling price | 50 | 68 | 94 |
| Material A | 20 | 30 | 40 |
| Material B | 5 | 8 | 10 |
| Labour | 10 | 5 | 15 |
|  |  |  |  |
| Demand (units) | 1,000 | 2,000 | 3,000 |

Material A is in short supply and ABC Co only have 10,000 kgs available. Material A costs $10 per kg.

What is the optimum production plan for ABC Co?

- ☐ 1000 As, 0 Bs and 2,975 Cs
- ☐ 0 As, 2,000 Bs and 3,000 Cs
- ☐ 1,000 As, 2,000 Bs and 500 Cs
- ☐ 1,000 As, 2,000 Bs and 3,000 Cs

---

8.12 KP makes 2 products, the K and the P.

|  | K | P |
|---|---|---|
|  | $ | $ |
| Selling price | 160 | 98 |
| Material C | 20 | 0 |
| Material D | 20 | 20 |
| Labour | 60 | 40 |
| Fixed costs per unit | 15 | 10 |

Labour is in short supply and KP have only 21,000 hours available per month. Labour is paid $20 per hour.

**What is the maximum contribution they can earn in the month?**

$ [                    ]

---

# 9 Linear programming

9.1 A clothing company manufactures jackets and trousers.

The inputs for the 2 items are as follows:

|  | Jacket | Trousers |
|---|---|---|
| Cotton | 3m | 2m |
| Polyester | 1.5m | 0.75m |
| Labour | 2 hours | 1.5 hours |

The maximum demand for jackets is 1,000, and for trousers 500 units. However, this does not include quantities ordered under a long term supermarket contract for 200 jackets and 50 pairs of trousers. The company would have to pay a substantial penalty if this were not satisfied.

All three resources are in short supply with maximum availability as follows:

Cotton 4,000m, polyester 2,000m, labour 2,800 hours.

There are not enough resources available to fulfil all of the demand and the contract units. In order to maximise contribution, the company is planning to use linear programming and needs to determine the constraints.

**The constraint formula for cotton is:**

- ☐ $3J + 2T \leq 3,300$
- ☐ $3J + 2T \leq 4,000$
- ☐ $3T + 2J \leq 4,700$
- ☐ $3T + 2J \leq 3,300$

---

9.2 **The definition of a shadow price is:**

- ☐ The premium that should be paid for one additional unit of scarce resource
- ☐ The premium that should be paid for additional resources where there is no slack of that resource
- ☐ The minimum that should be paid for one additional unit of scarce resource
- ☐ The contribution that can be earned from one additional unit of scarce resource
- ☐ The total that should be paid for one extra unit of scarce resource

BPP LEARNING MEDIA

9.3 A company has demand for 3 products as follows:

A 500 units
B 200 units
C 100 units

The resource requirements are shown below:

| | A | B | C |
|---|---|---|---|
| Labour hours | 2 | 1 | 4 |
| Material (l) | 3 | 7 | 2 |

The resources are limited to labour hours of 1,600 and material 3,500 litres.

**In determining the slack resources, which of the following is true?**

☐ There is slack labour
☐ There is slack material
☐ There is slack labour and material
☐ Both material and labour have no slack

---

9.4 Tall and Short Co manufactures two types of chair, the T and the S. The following information is available.

| | Chair T $ per unit | Chair S $ per unit |
|---|---|---|
| Selling price | 130 | 145 |
| Direct material | 25 | 30 |
| Direct labour | 40 | 50 |
| Variable overhead | 20 | 30 |
| Fixed overhead | 10 | 5 |

**If linear programming were used to calculate the optimum number of units to produce, which of the following would represent the iso-contribution line?**

☐ C = 35T + 30S
☐ C = 45S + 35T
☐ C = 30S + 35T
☐ C = 45T + 35S

---

9.5 **In order to solve a product mix decision where multiple constraints exist, place the following in the correct order (1 to indicate first step, 2 to indicate 2nd step etc) to show the methodology for determining the solution by the graphical method.**

| | |
|---|---|
| Define the variables | |
| Plot a graph | |
| Identify feasible area | |
| Plot iso contribution line | |
| Formulate constraints and objective function | |
| Determine optimal solution | |

BPP LEARNING MEDIA

### 9.6 Which of the following are assumptions of linear programming?

Select all that apply:

- ☐ Units of output are not divisible
- ☐ Total amount of scarce resource is known with certainty
- ☐ Fixed costs are unchanged by the decision
- ☐ There is no interdependence of demand between products
- ☐ Unit variable cost is constant

---

### 9.7 A clothing company manufactures jackets and trousers.

The inputs for the 2 items are as follows:

|  | Jacket | Trousers |
|---|---|---|
| Cotton | 3m | 2m |
| Polyester | 1.5m | 0.75m |
| Labour | 2 hours | 1.5 hours |

The maximum demand for jackets is 1,000, and for trousers 500 units. However, this does not include quantities ordered under a long term supermarket contract for 200 jackets and 50 pairs of trousers. The company would have to pay a substantial penalty if this were not satisfied.

All three resources are in short supply with maximum availability as follows:

Cotton 4,000m, polyester 2,000m, labour 2,800 hours.

There are not enough resources available to fulfil all of the demand and the contract units. In order to maximise contribution, the company are planning to use linear programming and needs to determine the constraints.

**The constraint formula for polyester is:**

- ☐ $1.5J + 0.75T \leq 1,662.5$
- ☐ $1.5J + 0.75T \leq 2,000$
- ☐ $1.5J + 0.75T \leq 2,337.5$
- ☐ $0.75J + 1.5T \leq 1,662.5$

---

### 9.8 A solution to a graphical linear programming problem showed that the optimal solution was found at the intersection of two constraint lines determined by the following set of simultaneous equations:

- $6x + 4y = 5,800$
- $14x - 10y = 5,800$

**Complete the following:**

The optimal number of product X =

The optimal number of product Y =

---

### 9.9 Product A sells for $140.

The cost card is:

|  | $ |
|---|---|
| Material X 2 m at $3 per metre | 6 |
| Material Y 3m at $8 per metre | 24 |
| Labour 3 hrs at $15 | 45 |
| Fixed overhead 3 hrs at 10 | 30 |

Material X in short supply and there is not enough to meet maximum demand. Material Y is not in short supply.

**Complete the following:**

The shadow price for material X is: $ [          ] per million.

Questions

9.10 A European directive has decreed that all companies should make more foods deemed to be 'healthy' than those deemed to be 'not healthy'.

**Which of the following correctly represents the constraint line to represent this directive on a graphical linear programming solution, where H = healthy and N = not healthy?**

☐ $N - H < 0$
☐ $N + H = 0$
☐ $H - N < 0$
☐ $N - H > 0$

---

9.11 **Which of the following activities would form part of a linear programming analysis?**

☐ Identify the feasible area
☐ Identify the drivers of cost
☐ Allocate costs to cost pools
☐ Identify the breakeven point
☐ Formulate the constraints

---

9.12 A company produces two products, the Wang and the Tang using the same resources. The company is determining the production plan for the period in the face of multiple resource constraints. Using linear programming it has been established that, at the point at which contribution is maximised, there are two resources used by the company that are binding constraints.

The binding constraints are formulated as follows where W and T represent the units of each product that can be produced:

Labour $\qquad$ $4W + 2T \leq 12,500$
Machine hours $\qquad$ $3W + 4T \leq 15,000$

**The number of units of Product Tang that can be produced under the optimal production plan is:**

☐ units.

---

9.13 B plc manufactures two types of boots, Knee High (K) and Ankle High (A). The following information is available:

| | Knee High | Ankle High |
|---|---|---|
| | $ per unit | $ per unit |
| Selling price | 40 | 30 |
| Direct material | 8 | 4 |
| Direct labour | 7 | 5 |
| | | |
| Variable overhead | 8 | 6 |
| Fixed overhead | 11 | 8 |

**If linear programming were used to calculate the optimum number of units to produce which of the following would represent the iso-contribution line?**

☐ $C = 15K + 17A$
☐ $C = 6K + 7A$
☐ $C = 17K + 15A$
☐ $C = 7K + 6A$

# 10 Forecasting techniques

**10.1** Which of the following components of a time series would be identified as a cyclical variation?

☐ Occasional peaks which occur unpredictably but on average once every five years.

☐ Regular cycles involving an increase in the first half of each year, followed by a corresponding decrease in the second half of the year.

☐ A peak in the first three years of every decade, with a corresponding trough in the last five years of every decade.

☐ An increase of the same amount each year over the last 50 years.

**10.2** BF Co manufactures a single product, and an extract from the flexed budget for production costs is as follows.

| | Activity level | |
|---|---|---|
| | 80% | 90% |
| | $ | $ |
| Direct material | 3,200 | 3,600 |
| Direct labour | 2,800 | 2,900 |
| Production overhead | 5,400 | 5,800 |
| | 11,400 | 12,300 |

The total production cost in a budget that is flexed at the 88% level of activity is:

$ [          ]

**10.4** For the linear equation $y = a + bx$, which of the following variable definitions is correct?

☐ y is the independent variable, whose value helps to determine the corresponding value of x.
☐ x is the dependent variable, depending for its value on the value of y.
☐ a is a constant, a fixed amount.
☐ x is the independent variable, whose value helps to determine the corresponding value of y.
☐ y is the dependent variable, depending for its value on the value of x.

**10.5** For some quarterly sales data, the trend has been calculated as increasing by 6 each quarter and the average seasonal variation for the 3rd quarter as - 22.5. The most recent data available is for the second quarter of Year 3 when sales were 370 units, and a centred moving average for the fourth quarter of Year 2 was 330.625 units.

**Using the additive model, predicted sales for the third quarter of Year 3 are?**

☐ 376 units
☐ 349 units
☐ 308 units
☐ 326 units

**10.6** The definition of a trend is:

☐ A medium-term change in results caused by circumstances which repeat in cycles.
☐ An underlying long-term movement over time in the values of the data recorded.
☐ A short-term fluctuation due to different circumstances which affect results at different points in time.
☐ A non-recurring fluctuation caused by unforeseen circumstances.

BPP LEARNING MEDIA

10.7 A sales analyst has established the following trend figures and seasonal variations for a company's sales:

| Quarter | 1 | 2 | 3 | 4 |
|---|---|---|---|---|
| | $'000 | $'000 | $'000 | $'000 |
| Year 7 | 1,500 | 1,528 | 1,552 | 1,530 |
| Year 8 | 1,557 | 1,580 | 1,608 | 1,632 |
| Average seasonal variation | −18 | +3 | +29 | −14 |

The analyst forecasts that the trend will increase by $25,000 per quarter in years 9 and 10.

**What is the forecast sales value for the first quarter of year 10 ($'000)?**

☐ 1,757
☐ 1,775
☐ 1,714
☐ 1,739

---

10.8 **When a moving average is plotted onto a graph, where should the plotted points be located?**

☐ At the end of the period to which they apply
☐ At the beginning of the period to which they apply
☐ At the mid-point of the period to which they apply
☐ Anywhere

---

10.9 By linear regression, the relationship between the monthly quantity produced (x) and total production cost (y) was found to be y = 15,000 + 286x.

**Estimate the variable production cost if output is 400 units.**

☐ $114,400
☐ $100,000
☐ $129,400
☐ $14,400

---

10.10 The following extract is taken from the production cost budget of L plc:

| Output | 2,000 units | 3,500 units |
|---|---|---|
| Total cost | $12,000 | $16,200 |

**The budget cost allowance for an output of 4,000 units would be:**

☐ $17,600
☐ $18,514
☐ $20,400
☐ $24,000

---

10.11 K Co has used regression analysis to determine the relationship between production costs and labour hours in its factory. The solution was determined as: y = 18,000 + 3x

Where

y = total monthly production cost
x = number of labour hours per month

In 20X7 production in January is expected to use 15,000 labour hours. After that, production levels will rise at a steady rate of 4% per month for the next two months, before stabilising for the remainder of the year.

**What are the expected production costs for the year 20X7?**

$ [          ]

10.12 Bing Co has the following cost information:

| | Month 1 | Month 2 |
|---|---|---|
| Production (units) | 250 | 300 |
| Costs ($) | 2,750 | 3,390 |
| Index | 110 | 113 |

All of the costs are variable.

**The monthly cost predicted for month 3 when production is anticipated to be 350 units and the index is predicted to be 114 is**

$ _____

---

10.13 **Which ONE of the following activities will be made possible if a company uses regression analysis to determine the trend of production costs?**

- ☐ Prediction of future costs for any future level of activity
- ☐ Analysis of past deviations from budgeted costs
- ☐ Prediction of future costs for activity levels within the company's relevant range
- ☐ Identification of the cause of an increase in costs

---

# 11a Budgeting for planning

11a.1 **What is another name for tactical planning?**

- ☐ Strategic planning
- ☐ Budgetary planning
- ☐ Operation planning
- ☐ Corporate planning

---

11a.2 **Which of the following are functional budgets?**

Select all that apply.

- ☐ Purchasing budget
- ☐ Cash budget
- ☐ Sales budget
- ☐ Marketing cost budget

---

11a.3 BDL plc is currently preparing its cash budget for the year to 31 March 20X8. An extract from its sales budget for the same year shows the following sales values.

| | $ |
|---|---|
| March | 60,000 |
| April | 70,000 |
| May | 55,000 |
| June | 65,000 |

40% of its sales are expected to be for cash. Of its credit sales, 70% are expected to pay in the month after sale and take a 2% discount. 27% are expected to pay in the second month after the sale, and the remaining 3% are expected to be bad debts.

**The value of sales receipts to be shown in the cash budget for May 20X7 is:**

$ _____

BPP LEARNING MEDIA

11a.4 **Which of the following definitions describe 'zero-based budgeting'?**

Select all that apply.

☐ A method of budgeting where an attempt is made to make the expenditure under each cost heading as close to zero as possible.

☐ Zero-based budgeting is a method of budgeting whereby all activities are re-evaluated each time a budget is formatted.

☐ A method of budgeting that recognises the difference between the behaviour of fixed and variable costs with respect to changes in output and the budget is designed to change appropriately with such fluctuations.

☐ A method of budgeting where the sum of revenues and expenditures in each budget centre must equal zero.

---

11a.5 **Put the following stages of an activity based budgeting system in chronological order.**

- 1st
- 2nd
- 3rd
- 4th

A   Take action to adjust the capacity of resources to match the projected supply

B   Determine the resources that are required to perform organisation activities

C   Estimate the production and sales volume by individual products and customers

D   Estimate the demand for organisational activities

---

11a.6 D plc operates a retail business. Purchases are sold at cost plus 25%. The management team are preparing the cash budget and have gathered the following data:

1   The budgeted sales are as follows:

| Month | $ |
|---|---|
| July | 100 |
| August | 90 |
| September | 125 |
| October | 140 |

2   It is management policy to hold inventory at the end of each month which is sufficient to meet sales demand in the next half month. Sales are budgeted to occur evenly during each month.

3   Payables are paid one month after the purchase has been made.

**The entry for 'purchases' that will be shown in the cash budget for September is:**

---

11a.7 The following statements have been made about rolling budgets.

1   Rolling budgets may be used to alter plans instead of encouraging managers to focus on improving performance.

2   Rolling budgets are not worth preparing unless there is a persistent and large amount of uncertainty about the future.

**Which of the above statements is/are true?**

☐ 1 only
☐ 2 only
☐ Neither 1 nor 2
☐ Both 1 and 2

11a.8 **Which one of the following weaknesses in a budgeting system is most likely to be found in a top-down system of budgeting?**

☐ Management budgets may include excessive amounts of 'slack' (unnecessary budget spending allowances)

☐ Management budgets may be too ambitious and beyond the realistic resource capabilities of the organisation

☐ Management budgets may not be realistic in practice

☐ Budgets may be inconsistent with the long-term strategy of the organisation

11a.9 **For which of the following reasons is budgeting more difficult in public sector organisations (such as government and the police force) than in private sector companies?**

Select all that apply.

☐ Difficulty in quantifying objectives
☐ Spending limits imposed by government
☐ Difficulty in quantifying outputs
☐ The public sector is larger than the private sector

11a.10 The following details have been taken from the receivables collection records of W plc:

| | |
|---|---|
| Invoices paid in the month after sale | 60% |
| Invoices paid in the second month after sale | 20% |
| Invoices paid in the third month after sale | 15% |
| Bad debts | 5% |

Customers paying in the month after the sale are allowed a 10% discount.

Invoices for sales are issued on the last day of the month in which the sales are made.

The budgeted credit sales for the final five months of this year are:

| Month | August | September | October | November | December |
|---|---|---|---|---|---|
| Credit sales | $80,000 | $100,000 | $120,000 | $130,000 | $160,000 |

**The total amount budgeted to be received in December from credit sales is:**

$ [            ]

11a.11 H Co is preparing the budgets for the forthcoming period.

In January it has sales demand of 5,546 units of finished product. Production has a wastage level of 6%. Inventories of finished goods are constant each month.

Each unit of finished product requires 2 litres of raw materials, at a cost of $1.50 per litre. Inventory levels of raw materials are planned to increase by 500 litres each month

**The materials purchases budget, in $, in relation to January's sales is:**

$ [            ]

11a.12 Oboe Co is preparing its budgets for the next month.

It has calculated that it needs to produce 11,875 units of finished product C, each of which required 4 labour hours to complete. There is unavoidable idle time in the factory due to production changeovers and it is currently running at 5%. The basic hourly rate for labour is $12. However if labour exceeds 40,000 hours in any one month this will be paid at time and a half.

**Calculate the labour budget, in $ for the period.**

☐ $598,500
☐ $600,000
☐ $657,750
☐ $660,000

---

11a.13 Bag Co has sales values for the first four months of the year as follows:

Jan $12,000
Feb $16,000
Mar $17,000
Apr $18,000

It is preparing its cash budgets and has noted the following past pattern of behaviour from customers:

20% of customers pay in cash at the time of the sale

50% of customers pay in the month after the sale, having been given a 1% discount to encourage prompt payment

15% of customers pay 2 months after the sale

10% of customers pay 3 months after the sale

5% of sales are written off as bad debts.

**Calculate the budgeted sales receipts for April.**

☐ $15,615
☐ $15,700
☐ $16,215
☐ $17,010

---

11a.14 **Match the budgeting terms provided to the definitions below:**

[          ] does not affect the optimal solution in a linear programming solution

[          ] is altered to reflect the actual level of activity

[          ] constrains what the business can achieve in the budget period

Picklist:

A bottleneck resource
A flexed budget
A non-binding constraint

---

BPP
LEARNING MEDIA

# 11b Budgeting for performance evaluation and control

11b.1 Cranberry manufactures a single product and has produced the following flexible budget.

| Activity level (units) | 10,000 | 12,000 | 15,000 |
|---|---|---|---|
| | $ | $ | $ |
| Direct materials | 20,000 | 24,000 | 30,000 |
| Direct labour | 50,000 | 60,000 | 75,000 |
| Production overhead | 45,000 | 50,000 | 57,500 |
| Admin overhead | 15,000 | 15,000 | 15,000 |
| Total | 130,000 | 151,000 | 177,500 |

**What would be the estimated total cost of producing 13,500 units?**

☐ $163,250

☐ $175,500

☐ $166,750

☐ $141,750

---

11b.2 **What is a budget cost allowance?**

☐ A budget of expenditure applicable to a particular function

☐ A budget allowance which is set without permitting the ultimate budget manager the opportunity to participate in setting the budget

☐ The budgeted cost expected for the actual level of activity achieved during the period

☐ A fixed budget allowance for expenditure which is expected every period regardless of the level of activity

---

11b.3 The production budgets for quarters 1 and 2 for a manufacturing company are as follows:

| | Quarter 1 | Quarter 2 |
|---|---|---|
| Production (units) | 5,000 | 7,000 |
| | $ | $ |
| Direct materials | 60,000 | 84,000 |
| Production labour | 52,000 | 65,000 |
| Production overheads | 70,000 | 70,000 |
| Total production costs | 182,000 | 219,000 |

**If the budgeted production volume for quarter 3 is 8,000 units, what will the total production costs be?**

$ ☐

---

11b.4 A Co uses a variety of computer models in its budgetary planning and control process.

Three of these models are described below.

**Which of these is/are a feedforward control model?**

☐ Model 1: An exponential smoothing model is used to prepare a forecast of sales volumes each month. If these forecasts indicate that budgeted sales levels will not be achieved, the marketing department is required to take appropriate control action.

☐ Model 2: An inventory control model is used to determine minimum and maximum levels for each inventory item. The model produces an exception report whenever the actual inventory level reaches minimum level or maximum level, so that control action can be taken if necessary.

☐ Model 3: A target is set for month-end cash balances. A spreadsheet model is used to forecast the net cash flow and the resulting cash balance for each month. Control action is taken if necessary to achieve the desired cash balance.

BPP
LEARNING MEDIA

11b.5 The costs of the factory maintenance department for JEB appear to have a variable element dependent upon the number of units produced. The fixed element of the costs steps up when 10,000 or more units are produced. At an activity level of 12,000 units, the fixed element of the cost is $15,000. The variable cost per unit is constant.

| Production volume | $ |
|---|---|
| 8,000 | 58,000 |
| 13,000 | 93,000 |

**The cost at 11,000 units of production is:**

$ _____

---

11b.6 The following statements have been made about flexible budgets.

1    Flexible budgets enable meaningful comparisons to be made between actual and expected revenues and costs.

2    In every variance reporting system which contains flexible budgets that compare budgeted and actual profit, there will be a sales volume variance.

**Which of the above statements is/are true?**

☐    1 only
☐    2 only
☐    Neither 1 nor 2
☐    Both 1 and 2

---

11b.7 Extracts from the flexible budgets of a manufacturing company are as follows.

| | 5,000 units | 7,000 units |
|---|---|---|
| Production and sales quantity | | |
| Budget cost allowance | $'000 | $'000 |
| Materials costs | 50 | 70 |
| Labour costs | 65 | 77 |
| Production overheads | 80 | 84 |
| Administration costs | 35 | 35 |
| Selling and distribution costs | 15 | 19 |
| Total cost allowance | 245 | 285 |

**What would be the total expenditure incurred in a period when 6,000 units are produced and 5,500 units are sold?**

Administration costs are 100% fixed costs.

☐    $234,000
☐    $250,000
☐    $263,500
☐    $264,000

---

11b.8 **Which TWO of the following statements apply to feedforward control?**

☐    It is the measurement of differences between planned outputs and actual outputs
☐    It is the measurement of differences between planned outputs and forecast outputs
☐    It is a proactive technique
☐    Variance analysis is an example

---

11b.9 XYZ Co is preparing the production budget for the next period. The total costs of production are a semi-variable cost. The following cost information has been collected in connection with production:

| Volume (units) | Cost |
|---|---|
| 4,500 | $29,000 |
| 6,500 | $33,000 |

**The estimated total production costs for a production volume of 5,750 units is nearest to:**

- ☐ $29,200
- ☐ $30,000
- ☐ $31,500
- ☐ $32,500

11b.10 **The original budgeted profit statement for a company, with all figures expressed as percentages of revenue, was as follows:**

|  | % |
|---|---|
| Revenue | 100 |
| Variable costs | 30 |
| Fixed costs | 22 |
| Profit | 48 |

However, it has now been realised that the sales volume will only be 60% of that originally forecast.

The revised profit, expressed as a percentage of the revised revenue will be:

- ☐ 20%
- ☐ 33.3%
- ☐ 60%
- ☐ 80%

# 12 Standard costing and variance analysis

12.1 **Which of the following statements about standard costing is NOT true?**

- ☐ Standard costing is useful where products are non standard or are customised to a customer's specifications
- ☐ Standard costing provides useful information to assist management in controlling costs
- ☐ Standard costing makes it easier to value inventory
- ☐ Standard costing can be used to predict future costs and set budgets

12.2 **Which of the following could explain why a favourable labour efficiency variance has arisen?**

- ☐ Workforce motivated to perform well with higher bonuses for efficiency
- ☐ Hiring of more highly skilled workforce
- ☐ Over absorption of overheads
- ☐ Out of date machinery resulting in delays in the production process
- ☐ Higher quality material purchased

12.3 Capacity levels used in setting standard absorption rates for production overheads are often related to performance standards.

**To which performance standard is budgeted capacity often associated?**

- ☐ Attainable standard
- ☐ Basic standard
- ☐ Ideal standard
- ☐ Current standard

BPP LEARNING MEDIA

12.4 **Which of the following correctly describes a standard hour?**

☐ An hour during which no machine breakdowns occur
☐ An hour during which only standard units are made
☐ An hour for which standard labour rates are paid
☐ The quantity of work achievable at standard performance in an hour

---

12.5 Fowell O'Durr plc manufactures the industrial insect repellent Wingblitz. Standard data for budgeted monthly production of 1,000 litres is as follows:

|  | Litres | $ |
|---|---|---|
| Chemical W | 700 | 1,400 |
| Chemical P | 400 | 600 |
|  |  | 2,000 |

Material inventories are valued at standard price, and inventories for the month of June were as follows:

|  | Chemical W Litres | Chemical P Litres |
|---|---|---|
| 1 June | 650 | 380 |
| 30 June | 650 | 295 |

During June, 670 litres of Chemical W were purchased for $1,474 and 320 litres of Chemical P at a price of $1.60 per litre. 900 litres of repellent were produced in June.

**What is the total direct materials price variance for June?**

☐ $162 Adverse
☐ $180 Adverse
☐ $163 Adverse
☐ $166 Adverse

---

12.6 **Which one of the following is the least likely reason why standard costs might not easily be applied to road haulage and distribution services?**

☐ It is difficult to measure labour times reliably
☐ Variable costs are negligible
☐ It is difficult to identify a standard item for costing
☐ Standard costing applies to manufacturing industries only

---

12.7 A company's sales budget includes 1,200 units of a product at a selling price of $200. Each unit has a budgeted contribution to sales ratio of 31%. Actual sales were 1,080 units at an average selling price of $180. The actual contribution to sales ratio was 34%.

**The sales volume contribution variance (to the nearest $1) is:**

☐ $7,440 A
☐ $8,160 A
☐ $24,000 A
☐ $21,600 A

12.8 **Which TWO of the following would help to explain a favourable material price variance?**

☐ An increase in the quantity of material purchased helped buyers to earn unexpected bulk discounts.

☐ Improved processing methods meant that material purchases were lower than standard for the output achieved.

☐ The material purchased was of a lower quality than standard.

☐ A decision to reduce the raw materials inventory during the period led to a reduced level of material purchases.

12.9 **What is the name given to a standard which has remained unchanged over the years and is used to show trends?**

☐ Basic standard
☐ Current standard
☐ Attainable standard
☐ Ideal standard

12.10 **Which of the following statements about setting budget targets is/are correct?**

1 Setting 'ideal standards' as targets for achievement should motivate employees to perform to the best of their ability.

2 Setting low standards as targets for achievement should motivate employees because they should usually achieve or exceed the target.

☐ 1 only is correct
☐ 2 only is correct
☐ Neither 1 nor 2 are correct
☐ Both 1 and 2 are correct

12.11 A company has an adverse idle time variance of $6,000 and the standard labour rate per hour was $3 per hour.

**If the actual hours worked were 12,000 hours, how many hours were paid for?**

☐☐☐☐☐☐☐

12.12 Spendthrift Co purchased 6,850 kgs of material at a total cost of $32,195. The material price variance was $1,370 adverse.

**The standard price per kg was $** ☐☐☐☐☐ **(to the nearest cent)**

12.13 During September, 300 labour hours were worked for a total cost of $4,800. The labour rate variance was $600 (A).

**What was the standard cost per labour hour?**

$ ☐☐☐☐☐

BPP LEARNING MEDIA

12.14 A company revises its standards at the beginning of each year. Because of inflation, it sets its standard price for materials at the estimated price level for the middle of the year. During a control period early in the year, a fairly large favourable direct materials price variance was reported.

**Which of the following would help to explain this variance?**

1    The control period was early in the year.
2    Direct materials were purchased in greater bulk than usual.

☐    Both 1 and 2
☐    2 only
☐    Neither 1 nor 2
☐    1 only

12.15 The following variances are extracted from the monthly management accounts of SG Co.

Direct material total variance                    $800 (A)
Direct material usage variance                  $1,200 (F)

**Which of the following statements is/are consistent with these variances?**

1    High quality material was purchased, which led to a lower level of quality control rejects of completed output.

2    Rapid inflation affected the price of the company's raw material so efforts were made to reduce the quantity of material used per unit of output.

☐    1 only
☐    2 only
☐    Both 1 and 2
☐    Neither 1 nor 2

12.16 A company made 60,000 items in 80,000 hours. The budget was to make 57,000 items in 82,650 hours.

**Will the fixed overhead capacity and efficiency variance be adverse or favourable?**

☐
| Capacity | Efficiency |
|----------|------------|
| Favourable | Adverse |

☐
| Capacity | Efficiency |
|----------|------------|
| Favourable | Favourable |

☐
| Capacity | Efficiency |
|----------|------------|
| Adverse | Adverse |

☐
| Capacity | Efficiency |
|----------|------------|
| Adverse | Favourable |

# 13 Further variance analysis

13.1    The following data relate to product Z and its raw material content for September:

Budget
Output                                11,000 units of Z
Standard materials content            3 kg per unit at $4.00 per kg

Actual
Output                                10,000 units of Z
Materials purchased and used          32,000 kg at $4.80

It has now been agreed that the standard price for the raw material purchased in September should have been $5 per kg.

**The materials planning price variance for September was:**

☐   $6,000 Adverse

☐   $30,000 Adverse

☐   $32,000 Adverse

☐   $33,000 Adverse

---

13.2   The following data relate to product Z and its raw material content for September:

Budget

| | |
|---|---|
| Output | 11,000 units of Z |
| Standard materials content | 3 kg per unit at $4.00 per kg |

Actual

| | |
|---|---|
| Output | 10,000 units of Z |
| Materials purchased and used | 32,000 kg at $4.80 |

It has now been agreed that the standard price for the raw material purchased in September should have been $5 per kg.

The materials operational usage variance for September was:

☐   $8,000 Adverse

☐   $9,600 Adverse

☐   $9,600 Favourable

☐   $10,000 Adverse

---

13.3   The standard material cost of one unit of product F is as follows.

| | | | $ per unit |
|---|---|---|---|
| Material G | 9 | litres × $4 per litre | 36 |
| Material H | 6 | litres × $2 per litre | 12 |
| | 15 | | 48 |

During March, 2,800 units of product F were produced, using 24,500 litres of material G and 20,500 litres of material H.

**The materials mix variance is: $** ☐ Adverse ☐ Favourable

---

13.4   The standard material cost of one unit of product F is as follows.

| | | | $ per unit |
|---|---|---|---|
| Material G | 9 | litres × $4 per litre | 36 |
| Material H | 6 | litres × $2 per litre | 12 |
| | 15 | | 48 |

During March, 2,800 units of product F were produced, using 24,500 litres of material G and 20,500 litres of material H.

**Complete the following statement.**

The material yield variance is ☐ Adverse ☐ Favourable

BPP LEARNING MEDIA

**13.5** Hardknott Co produces chemical NX57 by mixing two compounds. The standard material cost per unit of NX57 is as follows.

|  |  | $ |
|---|---|---|
| Compound C1 | 5 litres at $110.40 per litre | 552 |
| Compound C2 | 7 litres at $45.00 per litre | 315 |

During control period 13, the actual mix used was 1,098 litres of compound C1 and 1,350 litres of compound C2. Actual output was 200 units of NX57.

**What was the total material yield variance reported in control period 13?**

The total material yield variance reported in control period 13 is: $ [          ]   ☐ Adverse

☐ Favourable

---

**13.6** Two grades of labour work together in teams to produce product W. The standard labour cost of product W is shown below.

| Labour grade |  | $ per unit |
|---|---|---|
| 1 | 3 hours × $8 | 24 |
| 2 | 5 hours × $6 | 30 |
|  |  | 54 |

During February, 800 units of product W were produced using 2,550 hours of grade 1 labour and 4,090 hours of grade 2 labour.

**What labour mix variance arose in February?**

☐   $60 (A)
☐   $60 (F)
☐   $120 (A)
☐   $nil

---

**13.7** Two grades of labour work together in teams to produce product W. The standard labour cost of product W is shown below.

| Labour grade |  | $ per unit |
|---|---|---|
| 1 | 3 hours × $8 | 24 |
| 2 | 5 hours × $6 | 30 |
|  |  | 54 |

During February, 800 units of product W were produced using 2,550 hours of grade 1 labour and 4,090 hours of grade 2 labour.

**What is the labour yield variance which arose in February?**

☐   $202.50 (A)
☐   $1,620 (A)
☐   $1,620 (F)
☐   $1,740 (A)

---

**13.8** **In which of the following circumstances should the operational manager of a budget centre, rather than the purchasing managers, be held accountable for material price variances?**

1    When the operational centre uses excessive quantities of materials.
2    When the operational manager buys materials directly from suppliers.
3    When materials are purchased at short notice, at the urgent request of the operational manager.

☐   Circumstances 1 and 2 only
☐   Circumstances 1 and 3 only
☐   Circumstances 2 and 3 only
☐   Circumstances 1, 2 and 3

BPP LEARNING MEDIA

**13.9** **For which one of the following variances should a production manager usually be held responsible?**

☐ Material price planning variance
☐ Material price operational variance
☐ Material usage planning variance
☐ Material usage operational variance

**13.10** A company sells two products X and Y. Product X sells for $30 per unit and achieves a standard contribution of $12 per unit, which is 40% of the selling price. Product Y, a new product, sells for $80 per unit and achieves a standard contribution of just $10 per unit, which is 12.5% of the selling price. Budgeted sales are 5,000 units of X and 3,000 units of Y.

However the sudden cancellation of an advertising campaign for Product Y has meant that sales for the product will be well below budget, and there has been some price discounting in an attempt to obtain sales for the product.

**Which one of the following sales variances, if calculated, would you expect to show a favourable variance for the period?**

☐ Sales mix variance
☐ Sales price variance
☐ Sales quantity variance
☐ Sales volume variance

**13.11** RB makes product ABC which contains three ingredients. The standard costs of the product is as follows:

|  | Budget | Actual |
|---|---|---|
| Direct material usage: |  |  |
| Ingredient A | 50 kg per unit | 44,000 kgs |
| Ingredient B | 30 kg per unit | 31,000 kgs |
| Ingredient C | 20 kg per unit | 20,000 kgs |
| Production units | 10,000 | 9,000 |

**Which two sets of data will need to be compared in order to calculate the materials mix variance?**

☐

| Ingredient A | 44,000 kgs at standard price |
|---|---|
| Ingredient B | 31,000 kgs at standard price |
| Ingredient C | 20,000 kgs at standard price |

☐

| Ingredient A | 44,000 kgs at actual price |
|---|---|
| Ingredient B | 31,000 kgs at actual price |
| Ingredient C | 20,000 kgs at actual price |

☐

| Ingredient A | 47,500 kgs at actual price |
|---|---|
| Ingredient B | 28,500 kgs at actual price |
| Ingredient C | 19,000 kgs at actual price |

☐

| Ingredient A | 40,000 kgs at standard price |
|---|---|
| Ingredient B | 30,000 kgs at standard price |
| Ingredient C | 20,000 kgs at standard price |

BPP
LEARNING MEDIA

# 14 Risk and uncertainty in decision making

14.1    The owner of a van selling hot take-away food has to decide how many burgers to purchase for sale at a forthcoming outdoor concert. The number of burgers sold will depend on the weather conditions and any unsold burgers will be thrown away at the end of the day.

The table below details the profit that would be earned for each possible outcome:

| Weather | Number of burgers purchased | | | |
|---|---|---|---|---|
| | 1,000 | 2,000 | 3,000 | 4,000 |
| Bad | $1,000 | $0 | ($1,000) | ($3,000) |
| Average | $3,000 | $6,000 | $7,000 | $6,000 |
| Good | $3,000 | $6,000 | $9,000 | $12,000 |

**If the van owner applies the maximin rule he will purchase:**

- ☐   1,000 burgers
- ☐   2,000 burgers
- ☐   3,000 burgers
- ☐   4,000 burgers

14.2    The owner of a van selling hot take-away food has to decide how many burgers to purchase for sale at a forthcoming outdoor concert. The number of burgers sold will depend on the weather conditions and any unsold burgers will be thrown away at the end of the day.

The table below details the profit that would be earned for each possible outcome:

| Weather | Number of burgers purchased | | | |
|---|---|---|---|---|
| | 1,000 | 2,000 | 3,000 | 4,000 |
| Bad | $1,000 | $0 | ($1,000) | ($3,000) |
| Average | $3,000 | $6,000 | $7,000 | $6,000 |
| Good | $3,000 | $6,000 | $9,000 | $12,000 |

**If the van owner applies the minimax regret rule he will purchase:**

- ☐   1,000 burgers
- ☐   2,000 burgers
- ☐   3,000 burgers
- ☐   4,000 burgers

14.3 You are asked to interpret the following extract from a decision tree, which has been prepared for a decision that is to be made to choose between A, B and C.

**What is the maximum expected value of profit at decision point D?**

☐ $12 million
☐ $14 million
☐ $32 million
☐ $9.8 million

14.4 **A decision maker using the maximin decision criteria will:**

☐ Assume that they can ignore risk and will choose the outcome with the highest expected value.

☐ Assume that they will regret not having chosen another alternative and will therefore minimise the possible loss under this assumption.

☐ Assume that the worst outcome will always occur and will select the largest payoff under this assumption.

☐ Assume that the best payoff will always occur and will select the option with the largest payoff.

14.5 A company is considering the costs of a new product. The following table shows the predictions made for fixed costs and variable costs together with their associated probabilities for a particular output quantity.

| Fixed costs ($) | Probability |
|---|---|
| 100,000 | 0.40 |
| 120,000 | 0.35 |
| 150,000 | 0.25 |

| Variable costs ($) | Probability |
|---|---|
| 80,000 | 0.35 |
| 100,000 | 0.45 |
| 140,000 | 0.20 |

**The expected value for the particular output order quantity is: $** ☐

BPP
LEARNING MEDIA

14.6 A company is deciding which of four potential selling prices it should charge for a new product. Market conditions are uncertain and demand may be good, average or poor. The company has calculated the contribution that would be earned for each of the possible outcomes and has produced a regret matrix as follows:

*Regret matrix*

| Demand level | Selling price | | | |
|---|---|---|---|---|
| | $140 | $160 | $180 | $200 |
| Good | $20,000 | $60,000 | $0 | $10,000 |
| Average | $50,000 | $0 | $40,000 | $20,000 |
| Poor | $0 | $30,000 | $20,000 | $30,000 |

**If the company applies the minimax regret criterion to make decisions, which selling price would be chosen?**

- ☐ $140
- ☐ $160
- ☐ $180
- ☐ $200

14.7 **Which of the following statements about decision trees is/are correct?**

1 A decision tree can be used to identify the preferred decision choice using the minimax regret decision rule.

2 A decision tree is likely to present a simplified representation of reality.

- ☐ 1 only is correct
- ☐ 2 only is correct
- ☐ Neither 1 nor 2 is correct
- ☐ Both 1 and 2 are correct

14.8 A company is considering whether to develop and market a new product.

The cost of developing the product is estimated to be $100,000. There is a 70% probability that the development will succeed and a 30% probability that it will be unsuccessful, and the development costs will be lost.

If the development succeeds then the product will be marketed.

- There is a 50% chance that the marketing will be very successful and that profits of $150,000 will be made.

- There is a 40% chance that the marketing will be moderately successful and that profits of $50,000 will be made.

- There is a 10% chance that the marketing will be unsuccessful and that losses of $120,000 will be made.

The profit and loss figures take into account the development costs of $100,000.

**The expected value of the decision to develop and market the product is:**

- ☐ $83,000
- ☐ ($17,000)
- ☐ $58,100
- ☐ $28,100

14.9 A company can choose from 3 mutually exclusive projects. The net cash flows from the projects will depend on market demand. All of the projects will last only for one year. The forecast net cash flows, their associated probabilities and the expected values of the projects are given below.

| Market demand | Weak | Average | Good | Expected value |
|---|---|---|---|---|
| Probability | 0.40 | 0.30 | 0.30 | 1.00 |
| | | | | |
| Net cash flows | $'000s | $'000s | $'000s | $'000s |
| | | | | |
| **Project A** | 400 | 500 | 600 | 490 |
| **Project B** | 300 | 350 | 640 | 417 |
| **Project C** | 450 | 480 | 500 | 474 |

**The maximum amount that should be paid for perfect information regarding market demand is:**

$ [          ] 000

---

14.10 **A risk neutral decision maker will:**

☐ Ignore risk entirely in decision making
☐ Ignore risk when making decisions between projects that deliver the same expected value
☐ Avoid risk by trying to neutralise its impact
☐ Seek risk, because they are indifferent to risk

---

14.11 Production of aluminium tubes is normally distributed with a mean length of 50cm and a standard deviation of 5cm.

**What is the percentage of tubes (to 2 decimal places) that are at least 57cm long?**

[          ] %

---

14.12 A production manager has determined that when the equipment is working properly, the mean weight of items coming off a production line is 80kg. The standard deviation is 5kg.

An item has just been taken from the production line at random and weighs 84kg.

**What is the percentage chance (to two decimal places) that an item would weigh 84kg or more when the equipment is working correctly?**

[          ] %

BPP
LEARNING MEDIA

**14.13** **Which investment would a risk averse investor choose?**

- ☐ Project A
- ☐ Project B
- ☐ Project C
- ☐ Project D

**14.14** A supplier will supply company A in batches of 100 units, but daily demand is unpredictable. Company A has prepared a payoff table to reflect the expected profits if different quantities are purchased and in differing market demand conditions.

| Market conditions | Probability | Purchase 100 | Purchase 200 | Purchase 300 | Purchase 400 |
|---|---|---|---|---|---|
| Weak | 15% | 50 | (100) | (200) | (250) |
| Average | 25% | 120 | 120 | 250 | 100 |
| Strong | 50% | 90 | 200 | 300 | 400 |
| Exceptional | 10% | 80 | 300 | 400 | 500 |

**If the maximin criteria is applied, how many units would be purchased from the supplier?**

- ☐ 100
- ☐ 200
- ☐ 300
- ☐ 400

**14.15** A supplier will supply company B in batches of 100 units, but daily demand is unpredictable. Company B has prepared a payoff table to reflect the expected profits if different quantities are purchased and in differing market demand conditions.

| Market conditions | Probability | Purchase 100 | Purchase 200 | Purchase 300 | Purchase 400 |
|---|---|---|---|---|---|
| Weak | 15% | 50 | (100) | (200) | (250) |
| Average | 25% | 120 | 120 | 250 | 100 |
| Strong | 50% | 90 | 200 | 300 | 400 |
| Exceptional | 10% | 80 | 300 | 400 | 500 |

**If the maximax criteria is applied, how many units would be purchased from the supplier?**

☐ 100
☐ 200
☐ 300
☐ 400

---

14.16 A restaurant owner has correctly produced the following pay off table (containing total contribution values) for their decision of how many portions of the daily special to cook each day:

| Demand | Make 5 | Make 10 | Make 15 | Make 20 |
|--------|--------|---------|---------|---------|
| Poor | 20 | (10) | (5) | (20) |
| Average | 20 | 30 | 35 | 40 |
| Strong | 20 | 40 | 45 | 50 |

**Using the minimax regret technique, how many daily specials should the restaurant cook?**

☐

---

14.17 JB Co is launching a new product and there is uncertainty surrounding the level of fixed and variable costs. The following table shows the predictions made for fixed costs and variable costs together with their associated probabilities if 10,000 units are manufactured and sold for $70 each.

| Fixed costs ($) | Probability |
|-----------------|-------------|
| 20,000 | 0.40 |
| 30,000 | 0.35 |
| 40,000 | 0.25 |

| Variable cost per unit ($) | Probability |
|----------------------------|-------------|
| 60 | 0.35 |
| 55 | 0.45 |
| 50 | 0.20 |

**The expected value of the contribution for 10,000 is: $** ☐

BPP LEARNING MEDIA

14.18 You are asked to interpret the following extract from a decision tree, which has been prepared for a decision that is to be made to choose between A, B and C.

What is the maximum expected value of profit at decision point B? Provide your answer in $m and round to one decimal place).

$ [                    ]

14.19 A risk neutral investor has prepared the following table of profits to use when choosing between three investments.

| Investment | Good economic conditions $m | Average economic conditions $m | Bad economic conditions $m |
|---|---|---|---|
| 1 | 20 | 20 | 20 |
| 2 | 40 | 30 | 0 |
| 3 | 5 | 25 | 30 |

The probability of good economic conditions is 30%, average 50% and bad conditions is 20%.

What is the maximum the investor would be prepared to pay for a market research survey which could correctly predict the economic conditions?

$ [                    ] m

14.20 Bread Co has decided to start selling sandwiches which it will deliver to local offices daily. Demand is expected to vary between 125 and 200 sandwiches each day. As the day progresses, the price of the sandwiches is reduced and at the end of the day, sandwiches which have not been sold are thrown away. The company has prepared a regret table to show the amount of profit which would be foregone each day at each of the four possible supply levels.

|  |  | Daily supply of sandwiches (units) | | | |
|---|---|---|---|---|---|
|  |  | 125 | 150 | 175 | 200 |
| Daily demand | 125 | $0 | $11 | $41 | $60 |
| for sandwiches | 150 | $18 | $0 | $22 | $39 |
| (units) | 175 | $41 | $20 | $0 | $17 |
|  | 200 | $71 | $45 | $26 | $0 |

**Applying the decision criterion of minimax regret, how many sandwiches should the company decide to supply each day?**

☐ 125
☐ 150
☐ 175
☐ 200

# 15 Mixed Bank 1

15.1 The following statements have been made about the application of standard costing systems:

1   Standard costing systems are compatible with a Total Quality Management approach to operations.

2   Standard costing systems cannot be used in an industry that operates in a rapidly-changing environment.

**Which of the above statements is/are true?**

☐ 1 only
☐ 2 only
☐ Neither 1 nor 2
☐ Both 1 and 2

15.2 The budgeted contribution for HMF Co for June was $290,000. The following variances occurred during the month.

|  | $ |  |
|---|---|---|
| Fixed overhead expenditure variance | 6,475 | Favourable |
| Total direct labour variance | 11,323 | Favourable |
| Total variable overhead variance | 21,665 | Adverse |
| Selling price variance | 21,875 | Favourable |
| Fixed overhead volume variance | 12,500 | Adverse |
| Sales volume variance | 36,250 | Adverse |
| Total direct materials variance | 6,335 | Adverse |

**What was the actual contribution for the month?**

☐ $252,923
☐ $258,948
☐ $321,052
☐ $327,077

BPP LEARNING MEDIA

15.3 HG plc manufactures four products. The unit cost, selling price and bottleneck resource details per unit are as follows.

| | Product W | Product X | Product Y | Product Z |
|---|---|---|---|---|
| | $ | $ | $ | $ |
| Selling price | 56 | 67 | 89 | 96 |
| Material | 22 | 31 | 38 | 46 |
| Labour | 15 | 20 | 18 | 24 |
| Variable overhead | 12 | 15 | 18 | 15 |
| Fixed overhead | 4 | 2 | 8 | 7 |
| | Minutes | Minutes | Minutes | Minutes |
| Bottleneck resource time | 10 | 10 | 15 | 15 |

**If the company adopted throughput accounting and the products were ranked according to 'product return per minute', the highest ranked product would be:**

☐ W

☐ X

☐ Y

☐ Z

---

15.4 A company is considering the use of material X in a special order. A sufficient quantity of the material, which is used regularly by the company in its normal business is available from inventory.

**What is the relevant cost per kg of material X in the evaluation of the special order?**

☐ Cost of the last purchase

☐ Nil

☐ Replacement cost

☐ Saleable value

---

15.5 **When deciding, purely on financial grounds, whether or not to process a joint product further, the information required is:**

☐ The value of the common process costs

☐ The method of apportioning the common costs between the joint products

☐ The sales value of the joint product at the separation point

☐ The final sales value of the joint product

☐ The further processing cost of the joint product

---

15.6 W Co manufactures two products, the A and the B. The ratio of sales of A to B is 4:3. The following information relates to month 1.

| | A | B |
|---|---|---|
| | $ | $ |
| Selling price | 40 | 50 |
| Variable cost | 10 | 25 |
| Contribution | 30 | 25 |
| Fixed costs | | $975,000 |
| Budgeted sales revenue | | $2,000,000 |

**The margin of safety is:**

$ _____

15.7 The regression equation Y = 53X – 258 has been determined as a reliable estimate of Mac Co's deseasonalised sales (Y) in units for a control period X. Quarterly seasonal variations affecting Mac Co's sales levels are as follows.

| Q1 | Q2 | Q3 | Q4 |
|---|---|---|---|
| –20% | –30% | +5% | +45% |

**The forecast sales level to the nearest whole unit for control period 17, which is in quarter 3 is:**

| | units |
|---|---|
| | |

---

15.8 A company uses variance analysis to monitor the performance of a team of workers which assembles Product Q. Details of the budgeted and actual performance of the team for the last period were as follows:

| | Budget | Actual |
|---|---|---|
| Output of Product Q | 400 units | 490 units |
| Wage rate | $25 per hour | $28 per hour |
| Labour hours | 600 hours | 720 hours |

It has now been established that the standard wage rate should have been $27 per hour.

**What is the labour rate planning variance?**

- [ ] $1,200 (A)
- [ ] $1,470 (A)
- [ ] $1,200 (F)
- [ ] $1,470 (F)

---

15.9 The following statements have been made about standard mix and yield variances:

1 Mix and yield variances enable management to resolve problems with the quality of production output.

2 Persistent adverse mix variances may have an adverse effect on sales volume variances and direct labour efficiency variances.

**Which of the above statements is/are true?**

- [ ] 1 only
- [ ] 2 only
- [ ] Neither 1 nor 2
- [ ] Both 1 and 2

---

15.10 Nile Co is preparing its sales budget for 20X4. The sales manager estimates that sales will be 120,000 units if the summer is rainy, and 80,000 units if the summer is dry. The probability of a dry summer is 0.4.

**What is the expected value for sales volume for 20X4?**

- [ ] 96,000 units
- [ ] 100,000 units
- [ ] 104,000 units
- [ ] 120,000 units

BPP LEARNING MEDIA

# 16 Mixed Bank 2

16.1 The following statements have been made about standard costing:

1      Standard costing is well suited to organisations that produce items to customer specifications.

2      Predetermined standards conflict with a philosophy of continual improvement and total quality management

**Which of the above statements is/are true?**

☐    1 only
☐    2 only
☐    Neither 1 nor 2
☐    Both 1 and 2

---

16.2 **Which of the following statements are true?**

1      The fixed overhead volume capacity variance represents part of the over/under absorption of overheads

2      A company works fewer hours than budgeted. This will result in an adverse fixed overhead volume capacity variance

☐    1 is true and 2 is false
☐    Both are true
☐    Both are false
☐    1 is false and 2 is true

---

16.3 WTD Co produces a single product. The management currently uses marginal costing but is considering using absorption costing in the future.

The budgeted fixed production overheads for the period are $500,000. The budgeted output for the period is 2,000 units. There were 800 units of opening inventory at the beginning of the period and 500 units of closing inventory at the end of the period.

**If absorption costing principles were applied, the profit for the period compared to the marginal costing profit would be:**

☐    $75,000 higher
☐    $75,000 lower
☐    $125,000 higher
☐    $125,000 lower

---

16.4 CC Co is in the process of preparing a quotation for a special job for a customer. The job will require 510 units of material S. 420 units are already in stock at a book value of $50 per unit. The net realisable value per unit is $30. The replacement price per unit is $72. The material is in stock as a result of previous over buying. The units in stock could be used on another job as a substitute for 750 units of material V, which are about to be purchased at a price of $25 per unit.

**The relevant cost of material S for this special job for the customer is:**

$ [                    ]

---

**16.5** **When deciding whether or not to further process a joint product after the separation point the information required is:**

- ☐ The costs of the joint process
- ☐ The costs of further processing
- ☐ The quantity of losses expected from further processing and their sales value
- ☐ The sales value prior to further processing
- ☐ The sales value after further processing
- ☐ The quantity of losses that occurred during the joint process and their sales value.

---

**16.6** A clothing company manufactures jackets and trousers.

The inputs for the 2 items are as follows:

|  | Jacket | Trousers |
|---|---|---|
| Cotton | 3m | 2m |
| Polyester | 1.5m | 0.75m |
| Labour | 2 hours | 1.5 hours |

The maximum demand for jackets is 1,000, and for trousers 500 units. However, this does not include quantities ordered under a long term supermarket contract for 200 jackets and 50 pairs of trousers. The company would have to pay a substantial penalty if this were not satisfied.

All three resources are in short supply with maximum availability as follows:

Cotton 4,000m, polyester 2,000m, labour 2,800 hours.

There are not enough resources available to fulfil all of the demand and the contract units. In order to maximise contribution, the company is planning to use linear programming and needs to determine the constraints:

**The constraint formula for labour is:**

- ☐ $2J + 1.5T \leq 2,325$
- ☐ $2J + 1.5T \leq 2,800$
- ☐ $2J + 1.5T \leq 3,275$
- ☐ $1.5J + 2T \leq 2,325$

---

**16.7** Z plc has found that it can estimate future sales using time-series analysis and regression techniques. The following trend equation has been derived:

$y = 25,000 + 6,500x$

Where

y is the total number of units per quarter, and

x is the time period reference number.

Z has also derived the following set of seasonal variation index values for each quarter using a multiplicative (proportional) model:

| Quarter 1 | 70 |
|---|---|
| Quarter 2 | 90 |
| Quarter 3 | 150 |
| Quarter 4 | 90 |

**Using the above model, the forecast for sales units for the third quarter of year 7, assuming that the first quarter of year 1 is time period reference number 1 is:**

☐ units

BPP
LEARNING MEDIA

16.8 The following budgeted and actual sales information relates to a budget period for a company that makes and sells three products.

| Product | Budgeted sales Units | Budgeted profit per unit $ | Actual sales |
|---|---|---|---|
| X | 5,000 | 8 | 5,800 |
| Y | 3,000 | 14 | 2,700 |
| Z | 2,000 | 16 | 1,800 |

**What was the sales quantity variance for the period?**

☐ $1,000 (A)
☐ $3,240 (F)
☐ $3,800 (F)
☐ $8,550 (F)

16.9 A company makes and sells three products. Budgeted and actual results for the period just ended were as follows:

| Product | Budgeted sales units | Budgeted profit per unit $ | Actual sales units | Actual profit per unit $ |
|---|---|---|---|---|
| X | 800 | 10 | 700 | 8 |
| Y | 1,000 | 6 | 1,200 | 6 |
| Z | 600 | 12 | 350 | 16 |
| | 2,400 | | 2,250 | |

**What was the sales mix variance?**

☐ $1,475 (A)
☐ $1,475 (F)
☐ $1,800 (A)
☐ $1,800 (F)

16.10 The probability of an expected profit of $2,000 is 0.34, the probability of an expected profit of $1,850 is 0.15, the probability of an expected profit of $1,000 is 0.3 and the probability of an expected loss of $3,000 is 0.21.

**What is the probability of a profit of $1,000 or less?**

☐ 0.21
☐ 0.3
☐ 0.49
☐ 0.51

# 17 Mixed Bank 3

17.1 Which of the following statements are true?

1 A favourable fixed overhead volume capacity variance occurs when actual hours of work are greater than budgeted hours of work

2 A labour force that produces 5,000 standard hours of work in 5,500 actual hours will give a favourable fixed overhead volume efficiency variance

A    1 is true and 2 is false
B    Both are true
C    Both are false
D    1 is false and 2 is true

**Which of the above statements is/are true?**

☐    1 is true and 2 is false
☐    Both are true
☐    Both are false
☐    1 is false and 2 is true

17.2 The following data relate to Product D:

| | |
|---|---|
| Material cost per unit | $20.00 |
| Labour cost per unit | $69.40 |
| Production overhead cost per machine hour | $12.58 |
| Machine hours per unit | 14 |
| General overhead absorption rate | 8% of total production cost |

**What is the total cost per unit of Product D, to the nearest $0.01?**

☐    $176.12
☐    $265.52
☐    $286.76
☐    $300.12

17.3 A manufacturing company recorded the following costs in October for Product X:

| | $ |
|---|---|
| Direct materials | 20,000 |
| Direct labour | 6,300 |
| Variable production overhead | 4,700 |
| Fixed production overhead | 19,750 |
| Variable selling costs | 4,500 |
| Fixed distribution costs | 16,800 |
| Total costs incurred for Product X | 72,050 |

During October 4,000 units of Product X were produced but only 3,600 units were sold. At the beginning of October there was no inventory.

**The value of the inventory of Product X at the end of October using marginal costing was:**

☐    $3,080
☐    $3,100
☐    $3,550
☐    $5,075

BPP LEARNING MEDIA

**17.4** The following statements have been made about relevant costing:

1    Sunk costs can never be a relevant cost for the purpose of decision-making.

2    If a company charges the minimum price for a product or service, based on relevant costs, it will not improve its overall profitability.

**Which of the above statements is/are true?**

☐    1 only
☐    2 only
☐    Neither 1 nor 2
☐    Both 1 and 2

---

**17.5** A manufacturing company has the following monthly budget.

|  | $ | $ |
|---|---|---|
| Sales |  | 480,000 |
| Direct materials | 140,000 |  |
| Direct labour | 110,000 |  |
| Variable overheads | 50,000 |  |
| Fixed overheads | 130,000 |  |
| Total costs |  | 430,000 |
| Profit |  | 50,000 |

Sales can be increased by 15% per month if an extra work shift is added, but the sales price would have to be reduced by 3% on all units sold in order to sell the extra volume. Direct labour is a variable cost, but work in the extra shift would have to be paid an extra 50% per hour on top of the normal hourly rate. Increased materials purchase means that a 2% bulk purchase discount will be available on all material purchase. Additional fixed overheads would be $2,000 per month.

**If the additional work shift is added, what will be the monthly profit?**

☐    $51,400
☐    $52,150
☐    $53,410
☐    $60,060

---

**17.6** A company uses a standard absorption costing system. The following figures are available for the last accounting period in which actual profit was $210,000.

|  | $ |
|---|---|
| Sales volume profit variance | 10,000 adverse |
| Sales price variance | 7,500 favourable |
| Total variable cost variance | 9,000 adverse |
| Fixed cost expenditure variance | 5,000 favourable |
| Fixed cost volume variance | 3,000 adverse |

**What was the standard profit for actual sales in the last accounting period?**

$ ▢

---

**17.7** The following extract is taken from the production cost budget for K Co.

| Production (units) | 1,650 | 2,400 |
|---|---|---|
| Production cost | $20,770 | $23,170 |

**The budget cost allowance for an activity level of 1,980 units is:**

$ ▢

17.8 The following extract is taken from the production cost budget of L plc:

Output       2,000 units   3,500 units
Total cost    $12,000     $16,200

**The budget cost allowance for an output of 4,000 units would be:**

☐   $17,600
☐   $18,514
☐   $20,400
☐   $24,000

---

17.9 The following statements have been made about sales mix and quantity variances.

1     Sales mix and quantity variances are inappropriate for control report purposes when different managers have responsibility for sales of different products.

2     Sales mix variances can provide useful information for a company that wants to persuade customers to upgrade from a lower-cost and cheaper product to a higher quality and more expensive version.

**Which of the above statements is/are true?**

☐   1 only
☐   2 only
☐   Neither 1 nor 2
☐   Both 1 and 2

---

17.10 P Co currently sells 90,000 units of product Y per annum. At this level of sales and output, the selling price and variable cost per unit are $50 and $21 respectively. The annual fixed costs are $1,200,000. The management team is considering lowering the selling price per unit to $45.

The estimated levels of demand at the new price, and the probabilities of them occurring, are:

Selling price of $45

| Demand | Probability |
|---|---|
| 100,000 units | 0.45 |
| 120,000 units | 0.55 |

It is thought that at either of the higher sales and production levels, the variable cost per unit, and the probability of it occurring, will be as follows:

| Variable cost (per unit) | Probability |
|---|---|
| $20 | 0.40 |
| $18 | 0.60 |

**Calculate the probability that lowering the selling price to $45 per unit would increase profit.**

```
┌──────────────┐
│              │
└──────────────┘
```

BPP
LEARNING MEDIA

# 18 Mixed Bank 4

**18.1** Which TWO of the following are NOT features of a just-in-time (JIT) purchasing and production system?

☐ Maximum capacity utilisation

☐ Pull scheduling: buying or producing at each stage of the supply chain only when the next stage in the chain wants the output

☐ Kanban control: using a system of signalling work flow requirements using cards or other signalling devices

☐ Greater visibility of what is going on, such as open plan work place layouts and coloured lights to indicate stoppages

☐ Relying on a wide range of suppliers for raw materials and components, to ensure immediate availability of items

---

**18.2** A company manufactures two products: M and N. The company is considering changing the method it uses to allocate overheads to products and is looking at implementing an ABC system. Overheads are currently allocated based on labour hours.

|  | M | N |
|---|---|---|
| Production | 100,000 units | 150,000 units |
| Materials cost per unit ($) | 5 | 4 |
| Labour cost per unit ($) | 25 | 20 |
| Machine hours per unit | 3 | 2 |
| Number of production checks made | 200 | 600 |

Fixed overheads of $100,000 are split as follows:

| Machining | 30% |
|---|---|
| Set up costs | 40% |
| General admin | 10% |
| Checking | 20% |

Labour costs $5 per hour. Set up costs are based on the number of production runs and there is a new production run every 500 units. General admin allocation is based on units.

**Calculate which ONE of the following is the overhead allocated to one unit of product M under ABC.**

☐ $0.36
☐ $0.38
☐ $0.40
☐ $0.45

---

**18.3** If inventory levels have increased during the period, the profit calculated using marginal costing when compared with that calculated using absorption costing will be:

☐ Higher
☐ Lower
☐ Equal
☐ Impossible to answer without further information

18.4 A company makes and sells a single product. When sales per month are $6.8 million, total costs are $6.56 million. When sales per month are $5.2 million, total costs are $5.44 million. There is a step cost increase of $400,000 in fixed costs when sales are $6.0 million, but variable unit costs are constant at all levels of output and sales.

**What is the breakeven point for sales revenue per month?**

- ☐ $6.0 million
- ☐ There are two breakeven points: $5.64 million and $6.36 million
- ☐ $5.64 million only
- ☐ $6.36 million only

---

18.5 In a manufacturing plant, the work force is operating at full capacity. The work force is paid a fixed rate of $12 per hour for a 35-hour week. This is a fixed weekly wage, although for the purpose of management accounting, direct labour costs are treated as a variable cost. A customer has asked for a special job to be done that would involve taking employees off regular work that earns a contribution of $15 per hour, after allowing for direct labour cost and variable overheads at $3 per hour. The company must decide whether to agree to the customer's request for the work, and to set a price. The customers request is expected to take 10 hours.

**What would be the relevant cost of labour for this job?**

- ☐ $150
- ☐ $170
- ☐ $270
- ☐ $300

---

18.6 **Complete the following using the words below:**

BINDING
MAXIMUM
MINIMUM
CRITICAL
DETERMINANTS

Slack occurs when the [           ] availability of a resource is not used in the optimal solution.

Surplus occurs when there is production excess of a [           ] requirement. If there is no slack then the constraints are said to be [           ].

---

18.7 A shop has recorded its sales for the last 2½ years as:

| Year | Quarter | Sales |
|------|---------|-------|
| 1 | 1 | 300 |
|   | 2 | 320 |
|   | 3 | 275 |
|   | 4 | 280 |
| 2 | 5 | 340 |
|   | 6 | 355 |
|   | 7 | 300 |
|   | 8 | 300 |
| 3 | 9 | 360 |
|   | 10 | 370 |

**Using a centred annual moving average, the trend figure for the 1st quarter of year 2 is predicted as:**

- ☐ 317.50
- ☐ 315.63
- ☐ 340.00
- ☐ 312.50

BPP LEARNING MEDIA

18.8 **A flexible budget is:**

☐ A budget which, by recognising different cost behaviour patterns, is designed to change as volume of activity changes

☐ A budget for a twelve month period which includes planned revenues, expenses, assets and liabilities

☐ A budget which is prepared for a rolling period which is reviewed monthly, and updated accordingly

☐ A budget for semi-variable overhead costs only

18.9 **Complete the following using the statements below, to explain the importance of separating variances into their planning and operating components for the purposes of management control.**

Token (can use more than once):

ORIGINAL STANDARD
RELEVANT
REVISED
NOT CONTROLLABLE
CONTROLLABLE

Planning variances represent the difference between an ⬚ , which is no longer considered to be a ⬚ or accurate target, and a ⬚ standard. Planning variances therefore represent differences between target and actual performance which are ⬚ by operational management and so there is little to be gained from focusing management control action on such variances. An operating variance, on the other hand, represents the difference between a ⬚ , realistic target and actual performance and as such are deemed ⬚ by operational management. They therefore provide useful information for management control action.

18.10 A company expects to sell 1,000 units per month of a new product but there is uncertainty as to both the unit selling price and the unit variable cost of the product. The following estimates of selling price, variable costs and their related probabilities have been made:

| Selling price | Probability | Unit variable cost | Probability |
|---|---|---|---|
| $ per unit | % | $ per unit | % |
| 20 | 25 | 8 | 20 |
| 25 | 40 | 10 | 50 |
| 30 | 35 | 12 | 30 |

**There are specific fixed costs of $5,000 per month expected for the new product. The probability of monthly contribution from this new product exceeding $13,500 is:**

☐ 24.5%
☐ 30.5%
☐ 63.0%
☐ 92.5%

# 19 Mixed bank 5

19.1    **What are the advantages for a business of reducing greenhouse gases?**

☐    Distinguishing the business from its competitors
☐    Driving down energy costs
☐    Keeping the office illuminated after hours will increase awareness of the company
☐    Improving corporate reputation
☐    Attracting new customers who are looking for zero carbon footprint alternatives
☐    Warmer office environment making staff happier to stay longer
☐    Improving employee morale and employee performance

---

19.2    M Co is a furniture manufacturer. One of M Co's products is a chair which is produced in batches of 50.

Chairs go through 11 separate production processes which necessitate a total of 18 materials movements per batch.

There are 30,000 materials movements each year, costing $75,000.

**Calculate the activity based cost of materials movements per chair, to the nearest $0.01.**

$ ☐

---

19.3    One of the products manufactured by a company is Product J, which sells for $40 per unit and has a material cost of $10 per unit and a direct labour cost of $7 per unit. The total direct labour budget for the year is 50,000 hours of labour time at a cost of $12 per hour. Factory overheads are $2,920,000 per year.

The company is considering the introduction of a system of throughput accounting. It has identified that machine time is the bottleneck in the production process. Product J needs 0.01 hours of machine time per unit produced and the maximum capacity of the machine is 4,000 hours per year.

**What is the throughput accounting ratio for Product J?**

☐    3.41
☐    2.80
☐    2.10
☐    1.90

---

19.4    A company makes and sells three products. The budget for the next period is as follows:

|  | A | B | C |
|---|---|---|---|
|  | $ | $ | $ |
|  | per unit | per unit | per unit |
| Sales price | 12 | 18 | 20 |
| Variable cost | 3 | 6 | 11 |
|  | 9 | 12 | 9 |
| Fixed cost | 6 | 9 | 6 |
| Profit | 3 | 3 | 3 |
| Number of units | 30,000 | 40,000 | 10,000 |

**What is the breakeven point in sales?**

Give your answer in '000 to the nearest whole thousand.

$ ☐

---

BPP
LEARNING MEDIA

19.5 MM manufactures three components, S, A and T using the same machines for each and assembles them into a single product. The budget for the next year calls for the production and assembly of 4,000 of each component. The variable production cost per unit of the final product is as follows:

| | Machine hours | Variable cost |
|---|---|---|
| | | $ |
| 1 unit of S | 3 | 20 |
| 1 unit of A | 2 | 36 |
| 1 unit of T | 4 | 24 |
| Assembly | | 100 |

Only 24,000 hours of machine time will be available during the year, and a subcontractor has quoted the following unit prices for supplying components: S $29; A $40; T $34.

**Using the options below each component, select MM's most profitable plan.**

|  | S | A | T |
|---|---|---|---|
| Make | | | |
| | ☐ 4,000 | ☐ 4,000 | ☐ 4,000 |
| | ☐ 3,000 | ☐ 3,000 | ☐ 3,000 |
| | ☐ 1,000 | ☐ 1,000 | ☐ 1,000 |
| | ☐ 0 | ☐ 0 | ☐ 0 |
| Buy | | | |
| | ☐ 4,000 | ☐ 4,000 | ☐ 4,000 |
| | ☐ 3,000 | ☐ 3,000 | ☐ 3,000 |
| | ☐ 1,000 | ☐ 1,000 | ☐ 1,000 |
| | ☐ 0 | ☐ 0 | ☐ 0 |

19.6 DF Co produces a single product and currently uses absorption costing for its internal management accounting reports. The fixed production overhead absorption rate is $46 per unit. Opening inventories for the year were 100 units and closing inventories were 210 units. The company's management accountant is considering a switch to marginal costing as the inventory valuation basis.

**If marginal costing were used, the marginal costing profit for the year, compared with the profit calculated by absorption costing, would be which of the following?**

- ☐ $5,060 lower
- ☐ $5,060 higher
- ☐ $4,600 lower
- ☐ $4,600 higher

19.7 **When preparing a material purchases budget, what is the quantity to be purchased?**

- ☐ Materials required for production - opening inventory of materials - closing inventory of materials
- ☐ Materials required for production - opening inventory of materials + closing inventory of materials
- ☐ Opening inventory of materials - materials required for production - closing inventory of materials
- ☐ Opening inventory of materials + closing inventory of materials - materials required for production

19.8 A company's annual sales budget includes 2,250 units of a product at a selling price of $400. Each unit has a budgeted sales to contribution ratio of 29%. Actual sales were 2,445 units at an average selling price of $390. The actual contribution to sales ratio was 27%.

**The sales price variance to the nearest $1 is:**

- ☐ $24,450 A
- ☐ $22,500 A
- ☐ $24,300 A
- ☐ $26,406 A

**19.9** The following statements have been made about standard mix and yield variances.

1    Mix variances may be calculated whenever a standard product contains two or more direct materials.
2    When a favourable mix variance is achieved, there may be a counterbalancing adverse yield variance.

**Which of the above statements is/are true?**

☐    1 only
☐    2 only
☐    Neither 1 nor 2
☐    Both 1 and 2

---

**19.10** D provides a motorist rescue service to its members. It has been proposed to change the annual membership fee to $120 for the next year. The impact of this on the number of members is uncertain but the following estimates have been made:

| Number of members | Probability |
|---|---|
| 20,000 | 0.1 |
| 30,000 | 0.6 |
| 40,000 | 0.3 |

It is thought that the variable operating costs vary in relation to the number of members but the cost per member is uncertain. The following estimates have been made:

| Variable cost per member | Probability |
|---|---|
| $70 | 0.3 |
| $60 | 0.5 |
| $40 | 0.2 |

D expects to incur annual fixed costs of $1,100,000.

The management accountant of D has produced a two-way data table.

**Calculate the value that would be shown in that table in the cell for the profit from 40,000 members with a variable cost per member of $40.**

$ [            ]

---

# 20 Mixed bank 6

**20.1** **Which THREE of the following are particular problems of JIT?**

☐    It is not always easy to predict patterns of demand.
☐    JIT is a demand led system.
☐    JIT makes the organisation far more vulnerable to disruptions in the supply chain.
☐    Wide geographical spread makes JIT difficult.
☐    There is a risk that inventory may become obsolete.

---

**20.2** **Which of the following are activity based cost drivers used for?**

☐    Allocate overheads to resources.
☐    Reallocate service cost centre costs to production cost centres.
☐    Allocate overheads to cost objects.
☐    Allocate overheads to production and service cost centres.
☐    Allocate overheads to primary and support activities.

BPP
LEARNING MEDIA

**20.3** Last month a manufacturing company's profit was $2,000, calculated using absorption costing principles. If marginal costing principles had been used, a loss of $3,000 would have occurred. The company's fixed production cost is $2 per unit. Sales last month were 10,000 units.

**What was last month's production (in units)?**

☐　7,500
☐　9,500
☐　10,500
☐　12,500

---

**20.4** A company budgets to sells its three products A, B and C in the ratio 2:3:5 respectively, measured in units of sales. Unit sales prices and variable costs are as follows:

|  | A | B | C |
|---|---|---|---|
|  | $ per unit | $ per unit | $ per unit |
| Sales price | 20 | 18 | 24 |
| Variable cost | 11 | 12 | 18 |

Budgeted fixed costs are $1.2 million.

**What sales will be needed to achieve a target profit of $400,000 for the period, to the nearest $1,000?**

☐　$5.188 million
☐　$5.011 million
☐　$3.891 million
☐　$4.724 million

---

**20.5** A company has received a special order which will require 1 kg each of material X, material Y and material Z. Information relating to each material is as follows:

|  | X | Y | Z |
|---|---|---|---|
| Cost per kg of material currently in inventory | $90 | $60 | $140 |
| Current cost per kg | $100 | $70 | $150 |
| Refund available per kg | $80 | $nil | $100 |
| Cost of disposal if not used | $nil | $30 | $nil |

Material X is used regularly, whereas, the company has no further use for material Y and Z. The company currently has more than 100kg each of material X, Y and Z in stock.

**Calculate the minimum price for materials X, Y and Z in the special order:**

☐　$150
☐　$170
☐　$210
☐　$230

---

**20.6** A manufacturing company operates a standard absorption costing system. Last month 25,000 production hours were budgeted and the budgeted fixed production overhead cost was $125,000. Last month the actual hours worked were 24,000 and the standard hours for actual production were 27,000.

**What was the fixed production overhead capacity variance for last month?**

☐　$5,000 Adverse
☐　$5,000 Favourable
☐　$10,000 Adverse
☐　$10,000 Favourable

20.7  **Of what does the master budget comprise?**

☐ The budgeted statement of profit or loss

☐ The budgeted statement of cash flow, budgeted statement of profit or loss and budgeted statement of financial position

☐ The entire set of budgets prepared

☐ The budgeted cash flow

20.8  Cumberbatch Co operates a system of budgetary control involving the calculation of budget cost allowances. The following figures are produced for the month of April.

|  | Budget | Actual |
|---|---|---|
| Production units | 10,000 | 12,000 |
| Labour costs: All variable | $8,000 | $9,200 |
| Contribution | $29,000 | $32,900 |

**What conclusions can be drawn from April's figures?**

☐ There is a favourable variance on labour costs and contribution is higher than should have been expected.

☐ There is an adverse variance on labour costs, and contribution is higher than should have been expected.

☐ There is an adverse variance on labour costs and contribution is lower than should have been expected.

☐ There is a favourable variance on labour costs, and contribution is lower than should have been expected.

20.9  SW plc manufactures a product known as the TRD100 by mixing two materials. The standard material cost per unit of the TRD100 is as follows:

|  |  |  | $ |
|---|---|---|---|
| Material X | 12 litres @ | $2.50 | 30 |
| Material Y | 18 litres @ | $3.00 | 54 |

In October 20X3, the actual mix used was 984 litres of X and 1,230 litres of Y. The actual output was 72 units of TRD100.

**Calculate the total material mix variance for October 20X3.**

The total material mix variance for October is:

$ [          ]   ☐ Adverse   ☐ Favourable

BPP LEARNING MEDIA

20.10 The following decision tree shows four decision options: 1, 2, 3 and 4.

| | Probability | Benefit $ |
|---|---|---|
| 1 | 1.0 | 9,500 |
| 2 | 0.3 | 14,000 |
| | 0.3 | 10,000 |
| | 0.4 | 5,000 |
| 3 | 0.4 | 10,000 |
| | 0.6 | 9,000 |
| 4 | 0.7 | 8,000 |
| | 0.3 | 14,000 |

**Using the expected value rule, which choice should be made so as to optimise the expected benefit?**

☐ Choice 1
☐ Choice 2
☐ Choice 3
☐ Choice 4

# 21 Mixed bank 7

21.1 **A World Class Manufacturing manufacturer will have a clear manufacturing strategy aimed at which THREE of the following issues?**

☐ Meeting standard cost targets and avoiding variances
☐ Quality and reliability
☐ Flexibility
☐ Customer satisfaction
☐ Overhead recovery

21.2 F plc operates an activity based costing system to attribute its overhead costs to cost objects.

In its budget for the year ending 30 June 20X2, the company expected to place a total of 3,250 purchase orders at a total cost of $97,500. This activity and its related costs were budgeted to occur at a constant rate throughout the budget year, which is divided into 13 four-week periods.

During control period 10, a total of 267 purchase orders were placed at a cost of $10,146.

**What was the under recovery of these costs for control period 10?**

☐ $2,646
☐ $34,398
☐ $2,136
☐ Cannot be determined from the information provided

21.3 The following budgeted data has been prepared for a company that manufactures four products:

| Product | W | X | Y | Z |
|---|---|---|---|---|
| | $ per unit | $ per unit | $ per unit | $ per unit |
| Sales price | 9.0 | 6.0 | 4.0 | 8.0 |
| Variable cost | 5.5 | 4.0 | 2.2 | 4.0 |
| Budgeted sales units | 20,000 | 25,000 | 50,000 | 12,500 |
| Direct labour hours per unit | 0.5 | 0.25 | 0.3 | 0.8 |

**If the total available direct labour hours in the period is 24,000 hours and the company plans to maximise profit, which products should it make and sell in the period?**

☐ X, W and Y

☐ W, X and Z

☐ W, Y and Z

☐ Y and Z only

---

21.4 A company has fixed costs of $1.3 million. Variable costs are 55% of sales up to a sales level of $1.5 million, but at higher volumes of production and sales, the variable cost for incremental production units falls to 52% of sales.

**What is the breakeven point in sales revenue?**

Give your answer in '000 to the nearest whole thousand.

$ [            ]

---

21.5 **Which of the following are disadvantages of choosing to outsource part of the production process to a third party?**

(more than one option can be chosen)

☐ Loss of control

☐ No access to expertise

☐ Increase in capital required

☐ Loss of competitive advantage

☐ Loss of capacity

☐ Loss of in-house skill

---

21.6 Product A sells for $140.

The cost card is:

| | $ |
|---|---|
| Material X 2m at $3 per metre | 6 |
| Material Y 3m at $8 per metre | 24 |
| Labour 3 hrs at $15 | 45 |
| Fixed overhead 3 hrs at $10 | 30 |

Material X in short supply and there is not enough to meet maximum demand. Material Y is not in short supply.

**Complete the following:**

The shadow price for material X is: $ [            ] per m

BPP LEARNING MEDIA

21.7 **Which of the following could be used to describe activity based budgeting?**

Select all that apply.

☐ A method of budgeting based on an activity framework and utilising cost driver data in the budget-setting and variance feedback processes

☐ The use of costs determined using ABC as a basis for preparing budgets

☐ The definition of the activities that underlie the financial figures in each function and the use of the level of activity to decide how much resource should be allocated, how well it is being managed and to explain variances from budget

---

21.8 **Which of the following items should be included in the calculation of the sales volume profit variance?**

☐ Standard profit margin
☐ Actual profit margin
☐ Standard contribution margin
☐ Actual contribution margin

---

21.9 SW plc manufactures a product known as the TRD100 by mixing two materials. The standard material cost per unit of the TRD100 is as follows:

|  |  |  | $ |
|---|---|---|---|
| Material X | 12 litres @ | $2.50 | 30 |
| Material Y | 18 litres @ | $3.00 | 54 |

In October 20X3, the actual mix used was 984 litres of X and 1,230 litres of Y. The actual output was 72 units of TRD100.

**Calculate the total material yield variance for October 20X3.**

The total material yield variance for October is:

$ [          ]     ☐ Adverse     ☐ Favourable

---

21.10 A manager is deciding which of four potential selling prices to choose for a new product.

The estimated contribution depending on combination of selling price and demand is shown in the payoff table below:

| Selling price | $60 | $70 | $80 | $90 |
|---|---|---|---|---|
| Demand level |  |  |  |  |
|  | $'000 | $'000 | $'000 | $'000 |
| Excellent | 50 | 60 | 40 | 30 |
| Good | 40 | 50 | 30 | 20 |
| Weak | 20 | 35 | 20 | 10 |

If the manager applies the maximin criterion to make decisions, the selling price chosen would be:

☐ $60
☐ $70
☐ $80
☐ $90

# 22 Mixed Bank 8

**22.1** **In a TQM environment, which THREE of the following are likely to be prevention costs?**

- ☐ Performance testing
- ☐ Cost of repairs under warranty
- ☐ Administration of quality control
- ☐ Training in quality control
- ☐ Maintenance of inspection equipment

**22.2** JJ plc has recently introduced an activity based costing system. It manufactures three products, details of which are set out below.

|  | L | D | S |
|---|---|---|---|
| Budgeted annual production (units) | 200,000 | 200,000 | 100,000 |
| Batch size (units) | 200 | 100 | 50 |
| Machine set-ups per batch | 2 | 3 | 5 |
| Purchase orders per batch | 3 | 2 | 1 |
| Processing time per unit (minutes) | 4 | 5 | 5 |

Three cost pools have been identified. Their budgeted costs for the year ending 30 April 20X3 are as follows.

| Machine set-up costs | $270,000 |
|---|---|
| Purchasing of materials | $150,000 |
| Processing | $100,000 |

**The budgeted machine set-up cost per unit of product L is nearest to?**

- ☐ $0.54
- ☐ $0.15
- ☐ $15
- ☐ $30

**22.3** **Which of the following costing methods is most likely to produce useful information for decision-making?**

- ☐ Marginal costing
- ☐ Activity based costing
- ☐ Total absorption costing
- ☐ Standard costing

**22.4** A company makes and sells three products A, B and C. The products are sold in the proportions A: B: C = 1:1:4.

Monthly fixed costs are $55,100 and product details are as follows.

| Product | Selling price $ per unit | Variable cost $ per unit |
|---|---|---|
| A | 47 | 25 |
| B | 39 | 20 |
| C | 28 | 11 |

The company wishes to earn a profit of $43,000 next month.

**The required sales value of product A in order to achieve this target profit is:**

$ ☐☐☐☐☐☐☐☐☐☐

BPP LEARNING MEDIA

22.5 Lewis Co manufactures three products, K, L and G. Forecasted statements of profit or loss for next year are as follows:

| | K | L | G | Total |
|---|---|---|---|---|
| | $'000s | $'000s | $'000s | $'000s |
| Sales | 600 | 400 | 300 | 1,300 |
| Cost of production | | | | |
| Materials | (200) | (100) | (85) | (385) |
| Labour | (95) | (20) | (80) | (195) |
| Variable overhead | (75) | (10) | (20) | (105) |
| Fixed overhead | (250) | (120) | (80) | (450) |
| Gross margin | (20) | 150 | 35 | 165 |
| Selling costs | (30) | (20) | (50) | (100) |
| Net margin | (50) | 130 | (15) | 65 |

Fixed production overheads consist of an apportionment of general factory overheads, based on 80% of direct materials cost. The remaining overheads are specific to the product concerned. Selling costs are based on commission paid to sales staff.

As profits are low the senior management are considering stopping production of one or more of the products.

**Which product(s) should Lewis consider discontinuing?**

☐ Product K
☐ Product G
☐ Product K & G
☐ No product should be discontinued

---

22.6 Product A sells for $140.

The cost card is:

| | $ |
|---|---|
| Material X 2m at $3 per metre | 6 |
| Material Y 3m at $8 per metre | 24 |
| Labour 3 hrs at $15 | 45 |
| Fixed overhead 3 hrs at 10 | 30 |

Material X in short supply and there is not enough to meet maximum demand. Material Y is not in short supply.

**Complete the following:**

The shadow price for Material Y is: $ [          ] per m

---

22.7 **Which one of the following is NOT a common criticism of incremental budgeting?**

☐ It assumes that all current activities and costs are still needed.
☐ There is no requirement for managers to justify existing costs.
☐ There is no incentive for managers to reduce costs.
☐ There are no performance targets for managers.

---

22.8 Budgeted fixed overheads for cost centre 1 during the last accounting period were $75,000 for apportioned overheads and $95,000 for allocated overheads.

A pre-determined machine hour rate is used to absorb fixed overheads into product costs.

Budgeted machine hours during the period were 1,800.

Actual fixed overheads were $177,770 and the fixed overhead volume variance was $6,500 favourable.

**What was the fixed overhead total variance?**

Fixed overhead total variance is $ [          ] Adverse / Favourable

22.9  A standard product uses 3 kilograms of direct material costing $4 per kg. During the most recent month, 120 units of the product were manufactured. These required 410 kilograms of material costing $4.50 per kg. It is decided in retrospect that the standard usage quantity of the material should have been 3.5 kg, not 3 kg.

**What is the materials operational usage variance, if it is chosen to use planning and operational variances for reporting performance?**

☐  $270 (A)
☐  $240 (A)
☐  $40 (F)
☐  $40 (A)

22.10  A company has produced a payoff table showing the profit earned depending on a combination of the production and demand.

| Payoff table | Units produced | | |
|---|---|---|---|
| | 200 units | 210 units | 220 units |
| Demand | | | |
| 200 units | $12,000 | $11,600 | $11,200 |
| 210 units | $12,000 | $12,600 | $12,200 |
| 220 units | $12,000 | $12,600 | $13,200 |

**Complete the minimax regret table using the list of numbers below.**

$0
$400
$600
$800
$1,200

| Payoff table | Units produced | | |
|---|---|---|---|
| | 200 units | 210 units | 220 units |
| 200 units | | | |
| 210 units | | | |
| 220 units | | | |

BPP LEARNING MEDIA

# Answers to objective test questions

BPP
LEARNING MEDIA

# 1 Modern business concepts

1.1 The correct answers are:

- Achieving maximum capacity utilisation.
- Relying on a wide range of suppliers for raw materials and components, to ensure immediate availability of items.

JIT operations use pull scheduling, Kanban control and greater visibility in the work place. Pull scheduling (only producing for the next stage in the chain when the work is needed) results in a sacrifice of capacity utilisation. Supporters of JIT argue that it is better to be idle than to work on producing items for inventory. JIT purchasing systems rely on selecting a small number of reliable suppliers for key items, and involving these suppliers in the JIT planning and purchase ordering system.

1.2 The correct answer is:

A system which is driven by demand for finished products, whereby each component on a production line is produced only when needed for the next stage.

1.3 The correct answer is: Performance testing.

Performance testing is an appraisal cost.

Re-inspection cost is an internal failure cost. Administration of customer complaints section is an external failure cost and training in quality control is a prevention cost.

1.4 The correct answers are:

- Close relationship with suppliers.
- Minimal set up time and costs.
- Similar production time across all stages of the production process.

A close relationship with suppliers (so that raw materials are delivered as they are required), minimal set-up time and costs (so that small production runs are feasible) and similar production time of all stages of the production process (so that the speed of all processes matches the rate at which the final product is demanded by customers) are key requirements of successful JIT.

It does not matter whether raw materials are perishable or not (but if they are perishable, JIT is even more desirable).

1.5 The correct answers are:

- For standard costing to be useful for control purposes, it requires a reasonably stable environment;
- The ethos behind a system of standard costing is that performance is satisfactory if it meets predetermined standards;
- The control aspect of standard costing systems is achieved by making individual managers responsible for the variances relating to their part of the organisation's activities.

Cost and quality are important in a TQM environment.

If standards were set on an ideal basis, this would enforce the concept of continual improvement that TQM embodies.

In a standard costing environment, products or processes must be standardised and repetitive, so that standards can be established which will be useful for monitoring and control. In a total quality environment, however, continual improvements are likely to alter prices, quantities of inputs and so on.

Attainable standards, which make some allowance for waste and inefficiencies, are more common than ideal standards. The use of such standards conflicts with the elimination of waste which is a vital ingredient of a TQM programme.

1.6     The correct answers are:

- Absorption costing;
- Mass production

The CIMA *Official Terminology's* definition of WCM is a 'position of international manufacturing excellence, achieved by developing a culture based on factors such as continuous improvement, problem prevention, zero defect tolerance, customer-driven JIT-based production and total quality management.'

Absorption costing and mass production would not be associated with such aims.

1.7     The correct answer is:

Physical information about the use and flows of energy, water and materials, including waste and emissions.

Environmental management accounting measures physical quantities as well as monetary amounts. Management accounting is concerned with providing information to management, not with external reporting to shareholders.

# 2 Environmental costing

2.1     The correct answers are:

- Reducing energy consumption
- Increasing use of renewable electricity
- Offsetting

Using more energy from the national grid/country's central supply will actually increase the carbon consumed by the organisation.

2.2     The correct answers are:

| Cost | Classification |
|------|----------------|
| Repairs under warranty | B |
| Inspection of goods in | C |
| Product design | D |
| Lower selling price for sub quality goods | A |

2.3     The correct answers are:

- Cleaning up contaminated soil
- Government penalties and fines

Environmental external failure costs are costs arising when the business releases harmful waste into the environment

2.4     The correct answer is: Both 1 and 2.

A system of environmental management accounting provides environmental information for internal use by management, but not for external reporting. It is distinct from environmental accounting, which is concerned with external reporting (as well as internal reporting). Environmental management accounting systems typically make use of life cycle costing, given that there may be substantial clean-up and disposal costs at the end of the life of an activity or operation.

BPP LEARNING MEDIA

# 3a Absorption costing

**3a.1** The correct answer is: $0.55.

Different newspapers require different labour hours and machine hours as they are not identical.

Using a labour hour rate is not appropriate as production is more machine intensive than labour intensive. A machine hour is therefore more appropriate.

Number of machine hours = (60,000 × 0.4) + (80,000 × 0.5) + (90,000 × 0.3) = 91,000

Absorption rate = ($24,570 + $25,730) ÷ 91,000 hours = $0.55 per machine hour.

Distribution costs have been excluded as these are a non-production cost.

**3a.2** The correct answer is:

Actual overheads incurred are lower than the amount absorbed.

Over-absorption occurs when the overhead absorbed is greater than the actual overhead amount incurred. In other words, the actual overheads incurred are lower than the amount absorbed.

**3a.3** The correct answer is: (i) and (ii) only.

Statement (i) is correct because a constant unit absorption rate is used throughout the period.

Statement (ii) is correct because 'actual' overhead costs, based on actual overhead expenditure and actual activity for the period, cannot be determined until after the end of the period.

Statement (iii) is incorrect because under/over absorption of overheads is caused by the use of predetermined overhead absorption rates.

**3a.4** The correct answer is: $30,000.

|  | $ |
|---|---|
| Actual fixed production overheads | X |
| Absorbed fixed production overheads (4,500 × $8) | 36,000 |
| Over-absorbed fixed production overheads | 6,000 |

Actual fixed production overheads = $36,000 − $6,000
= $30,000

**3a.5** The correct answer is: 240,000 units.

The total fixed production overhead variance ($100,000 Adverse) is the difference between fixed overhead incurred and fixed overhead absorbed (the under or over-absorbed fixed overhead.)

$$\$100,000 \text{ Adverse} = \$1,300,000 - (\$\left(\frac{1,000,000}{200,000}\right) * \times \text{actual level of production})$$

$$* \frac{1,000,000}{200,000} = \text{standard overhead absorption rate}$$

$$100,000 = 1,300,000 - ( 5 \times \text{actual level of production})$$

$$\frac{1,300,000 - 100,000}{5} = \text{actual production}$$

$$= \frac{1,200,000}{5} = 240,000 \text{ units}$$

**3a.6** The correct answer is: $10,000 over absorbed.

| OAR for last year | = Budgeted overheads/Budgeted machine hours |
|---|---|
|  | = $660,000/44,000 hours |
|  | = $15 per hour |
| OAR per unit | = $15 per hour × 0.2 hours/unit = $3 |

Overheads absorbed        = 200,000 × $3
                          = $600,000
Actual overheads          = $590,000

∴ overheads were over absorbed by $590,000-$600,000

= $10,000 over absorption

3a.7    The correct answer is: $117,400.

Absorption costing:

OAR = Budgeted overhead / budgeted production = $130,000/25,000 = $5.2/unit

As inventory has increased, absorption costing will report a higher profit than marginal costing.

The difference in profit        = change in inventory volume × fixed production overhead rate per unit
                                = 2,000 × $5.2
                                = $10,400
Marginal profit                 = $107,000 (W1)
∴ Absorption profit             = $107,000 + $10,400 = $117,400

Working 1:

|  | $'000 |
|---|---|
| Total contribution (20,000 × $15) | 300 |
| Less fixed production overhead | (118) |
| Less fixed selling costs | (75) |
| MC profit | 107 |

3a.8    The correct answer is: Absorbed overheads exceed actual overheads.

Absorbed overheads exceed budgeted overheads – could lead to under-absorbed overheads if actual overheads far exceeded both budgeted overheads and the overhead absorbed.

If actual overheads exceed absorbed overheads then we have under-absorption.

3a.9    The correct answer is: $20,700

Units sold = units produced + opening units - closing units = 5,000 + 400 - 900 = 4,500 units

4,500 units × $4.60 = $20,700

Or

|  | $ | $ |
|---|---|---|
| Sales (4,500 × $20) |  | 90,000 |
| Less cost of sales |  |  |
| Opening inv (400 × $15.4) | 6,160 |  |
| Purchases (5,000 × $15.4) | 77,000 |  |
| Less closing inv (900 × $15.4) | (13,860) | (69,300) |
| Gross profit |  | 20,700 |

3a.10   The correct answer is: $78,000 over absorbed.

In a standard absorption costing system, overheads are absorbed based on the standard content of actual output.

$$OAR = \frac{Budgeted\,fixed\,overheads}{Budgeted\,level\,of\,activity}$$

$$= \frac{\$540,000}{1,080,000}$$

$$= \$0.50 \text{ per labour hour}$$

BPP
LEARNING MEDIA

Absorbed overheads = OAR × standard content of actual output

72,000 units × 18 hours = 1,296,000 standard hours

Absorbed overheads = $0.50 × 1,296,000 = $648,000
Incurred overheads                  $570,000
Therefore over absorption       $78,000

# 3b Activity based costing

**3b.1** The correct answer is: Number of set ups.

**3b.2** The correct answer is: $31.42.

| Overhead (a) | Total number of cost driver units (W1) | Cost driver rate (a) ÷ (b) = (c) | Overhead absorbed for unit X (W2) |
|---|---|---|---|
| $488,000 | 61,000 machine hours | $8 | $288,000 |
| $85,000 | 50 set-ups | $1,700 | $17,000 |
| $162,000 | 36 orders | $4,500 | $72,000 |
| | | | $377,000 |

Amount absorbed per unit = $377,000/12,000 = $31.42

Working

1     (12,000 × 3) + (25,000 × 1) = 61,000 machine hours
       10 + 40 = 50 set-ups
       16 + 20 = 36 orders

2     $8 × 12,000 × 3 = $288,000
       $1,700 × 10 = $17,000
       $4,500 × 16 = $72,000

**3b.3** The correct answer is: (iii) and (iv).

ABC is an alternative to traditional volume-based costing models, where production overhead is absorbed on the basis of the volume of direct labour hours or machine hours worked. However, it is still a form of absorption costing because production overheads are absorbed in product costs. (The difference is the use of multiple OARs.)

ABC can be used for costing services as well as products and although it looks at the cost of activities, it is not a method for identifying relevant costs for short-term decision making. However, by identifying cost drivers it can help to influence long-term decision making.

**3b.4** The correct answer is: $58,500.

Total contribution = $8,100,000 + $1,000,000 = $9,100,000.

Contribution per unit = $9,100,000/130,000 = $70.

| Cost pool | Overhead ($) | Cost per cost driver |
|---|---|---|
| Order processing | 250,000 | $5 per order |
| Sales force salaries | 400,000 | $20 per hour |
| Research | 350,000 | $35 per hour |

Customer X overhead = ($5 × 400) + ($20 × 300) + ($35 × 100) = $11,500

Customer X contribution = $70,000

Customer X profit = $70,000 - $11,500 = $58,500

3b.5    The correct answer is: I, III and IV.

I       Short-term variable overhead costs should be traced to products using volume-related cost drivers, such as machine hours or direct labour hours.

        Correct. Short-term variable overhead costs vary with the volume of activity, and should be allocated to products accordingly.

II      Long-term variable production overhead costs are driven partly by the complexity and diversity of production work, as well as by the volume of output.

        This statement is not completely correct. Many overhead costs, traditionally regarded as fixed costs, vary in the long run with the volume of certain activities, although they do not vary immediately. The activities they vary with are principally related to the complexity and diversity of production, not to sheer volume of output. For example, set-up costs vary in the long run with the number of production runs scheduled, not the number of units produced.

III     Transactions undertaken by support department personnel are the appropriate cost drivers for long-term variable overhead costs.

        Correct. For example, the number of credit investigations undertaken within the credit review department of a bank would be the cost driver of the department's costs.

IV      Overheads should be charged to products on the basis of their usage of an activity. A product's usage of an activity is measured by the number of the activity's cost driver it generates.

        Correct. A mortgage might require three credit investigations and hence the mortgage should bear a proportion of the departments' costs to reflect the three credit investigations.

3b.6    The correct answer is: $112.91.

Rate per cost driver

| | | |
|---|---|---|
| Machining | $35,750/12,500 machine hours | = $2.86 per machine hour |
| Set-up costs | $5,250/10 production runs | = $525 per run |
| Materials handling | $17,500/40 materials deliveries | = $437.50 per delivery |
| Packing costs | $22,500/15 deliveries to customers | = $1,500 per delivery |

| Product Y overhead costs | | $ |
|---|---|---|
| Machining | 2,000 machine hours × $2.86 | 5,720.00 |
| Set-up costs | 2 prod runs × $525 | 1,050.00 |
| Materials handling | 19 deliveries × $437.50 | 8,312.50 |
| Packing costs | 5 customer deliveries × $1,500 | 7,500.00 |
| | | 22,582.50 |

Overhead cost per unit = $22,582.50/200 units = $112.91

If you answered $2.86, this is the rate per machine hour.

If you answered $525, this is the rate per set-up.

If you answered $150.55, this is product Y's overhead costs divided by product Z volume.

3b.7    The correct answer is: ABC identifies value added and non-value added activities.

The results of ABC must be interpreted by management before they can be used to identify which activities add value and which do not.

The other statements explain why ABC gives more accurate information than traditional absorption costing.

3b.8    **The correct answer is: $0.54.**

$$OAR = \frac{\text{Annual machine set-up costs}}{\text{Total number of set-ups}}$$

Total number of set-ups = number of batches × set-ups per batch

BPP
LEARNING MEDIA

|            |                        | Batches   | Set-ups |
|------------|------------------------|-----------|---------|
| Product A  | $\dfrac{80,000}{100}$ = | 800 × 3   | 2,400   |
| Product B  | $\dfrac{100,000}{50}$ = | 2,000 × 4 | 8,000   |
| Product C  | $\dfrac{50,000}{25}$ =  | 2,000 × 6 | 12,000  |
|            |                        |           | 22,400  |

$$\text{OAR} = \frac{\$150,000}{22,400} = \$6.70 \text{ per set up}$$

Product B has 8,000 set-ups so total cost for Product B = $6.70 × 8,000 = $53,600

Cost per unit of B = $53,600 / 100,000 units = $0.54

**3b.9** The correct answer is: $120.

$$\text{OAR} = \frac{\text{Material handling costs}}{\text{Number of batches}}$$

|   |                        | Batches |
|---|------------------------|---------|
| X | $\dfrac{50,000}{250}$ = | 200     |
| Y | $\dfrac{25,000}{100}$ = | 250     |
| Z | $\dfrac{20,000}{400}$ = | 50      |
|   |                        | 500     |

$$\text{OAR} = \frac{\$60,000}{500} = \$120 \text{ per batch}$$

**3b.10** The correct answers are:

| Purchase order processing costs | A |
|---------------------------------|---|
| Product advertising costs       | B |
| Factory rent and rates          | C |
| Direct labour costs             | D |
| Product redesign costs          | B |
| Material handling costs         | A |

**3b.11** The correct answer is: $47.

| Production set up cost | = $134,400/7 | = $19,200 per set up     |
|------------------------|--------------|--------------------------|
| Quality control costs  | = $55,200/9  | = $6,133.3 per inspection |

Total overheads for Tickles:

| Set ups     | 2 × $19,200   | = $38,400 |
|-------------|---------------|-----------|
| Inspections | 6 × $6,133.3  | = $36,800 |
|             |               | $75,200   |

Per unit:

$75,200/1,600 units = $47 per unit.

# 4 Marginal costing and throughput accounting

4.1    The correct answer is: absorption costing profits would be higher by $27,000

Difference between absorption costing profits and marginal costing profits = difference between opening and closing inventory levels × fixed overhead absorbed per unit

| Closing inventory | = opening inventory + production – sales |
|---|---|
|  | = 980 + 13,250 – 12,500 |
|  | = 1,730 units |
| ∴ Difference in profits | = (1,730 – 980) × $36 = $27,000 |

Closing inventory is greater than opening inventory which means some fixed overhead has been carried forward to be charged against the next period's profit under absorption costing.

∴ Absorption costing profit is greater than marginal costing profit.

4.2    The correct answer is: $107 ('000)

MC profit

|  | $'000 |
|---|---|
| Total contribution (20,000 × $15) | 300 |
| Less fixed production overhead | (118) |
| Less fixed selling costs | (75) |
| MC profit | 107 |

4.3    The correct answer is:

- Work in progress is valued at material cost only.

The other options are incorrect because:

- Work in progress is valued at material cost only
- Material cost is added to products during production
- Only material cost is treated as a variable cost.

4.4    The correct answer is: Machine 2.

Machine 2 is the bottleneck machine as it has the highest utilisation of all three machines at 154%.

Utilisation rates:

| Machine 1 (440/400) | = 110% |
|---|---|
| Machine 2 (615/400) | = 154% |
| Machine 3 (205/400) | = 51% |

Max time required on machine 1: (5 × 50) + (2 × 50) + (1.5 × 60) = 440 hours

Max time required on machine 2: (5 × 50) + (5.5 × 50) + (1.5 × 60) = 615 hours

Max time required on machine 3: (2.5 × 50) + (1 × 50) + (0.5 × 60) = 205 hours

4.5    The correct answer is: 1 and 2

Statement 3 is incorrect as the shadow price is the maximum **extra** amount paid for one additional unit.

4.6    The correct answer is: $180,000 lower.

| | Units |
|---|---|
| Opening inventory | 1,800 |
| Closing inventory | 900 |
| Decrease | |

$$900 \times \left( \frac{\$400,000}{2,000} \right)$$

= $180,000 lower

**4.7** The correct answer is:

None of the above statements are true.

The product with the highest TA ratio should be produced first.

**4.8** The correct answer is:

Absorption costing profits will be higher and closing inventory valuations higher than those under marginal costing.

Closing inventory valuation under absorption costing will always be higher than under marginal costing because of the absorption of fixed overheads into closing inventory values.

The profit under absorption costing will be greater because the fixed overhead being carried forward in closing inventory is greater than the fixed overhead being written off in opening inventory.

**4.9** The correct answer is: $415,000.

Total contribution from each unit of service of X, Y and Z = $40 + $70 + $25 = $135

If equal quantities of X, Y and Z are sold, total contribution required to cover fixed costs and result in $40,000 profit is $140,000 ( = desired profit + fixed cost).

Therefore: $\dfrac{\text{Total contribution required}}{\text{Contribution per unit of X, Y, Z}} = \dfrac{\$140,000}{\$135} = 1,037$ units of each X, Y, and Z

Sales value of one unit of each service is $100 + $200 + $100 = $400

Sales value required = $400 × 1,037 = $414,800

**4.10** The correct answer is: (ii) and (iii)

The mark up used for both is arbitrary to an extent as it does not take into account external factors, such as the level of competition or the market conditions. Often a firm will adjust the final selling price to reflect such conditions.

The price elasticity of demand looks at the responsiveness of demand to a change in the price. Combining the revised level of demand and selling price it is possible to evaluate the impact on total revenue.

**4.11** The correct answer is: None of them

It is actually a mark-up which will give a higher percentage for the same product. For example a 33% mark-up is the same as a 25% margin, meaning the first statement is false.

Using full cost pricing will only ensure that a profit is generated if the predicted level of overheads and volume of activity is correct.

Marginal costing applies similar principles to relevant costing, because it is based on variable costs. The reason it is not a form of relevant costing is that adding a profit margin/mark-up is an accounting adjustment and not a relevant cost.

# 5 Limiting factor analysis

**5.1** The correct answer is: B.

| | X | Y | Z |
|---|---|---|---|
| | $ per unit | $ per unit | $ per unit |
| Selling price | 75 | 95 | 96 |
| Variable cost | 34 | 41 | 45 |
| Contribution | 41 | 54 | 51 |
| Kg of material used per unit | 2 | 1 | 3 |
| Contribution per kg | $20.50 | $54 | $17 |
| Ranking | 2 | 1 | 3 |

If you chose option A, you ranked according to unit contribution.

If you chose option C, you ranked according to selling price.

If you chose option D, you ranked according to usage of material.

5.2    The correct answer is: $2,240.

Limiting factor is raw material.

|  | M | N | P |
|---|---|---|---|
| **Contribution per kg of limiting factor** | | | |
| $4.50/($1.25 ÷ $0.50) | $1.80 | | |
| $4.80/($1.50 ÷ $0.50) | | $1.60 | |
| $2.95/($0.75 ÷ $0.50) | | | $1.97 |
| **Ranking** | 2 | 3 | 1 |

**Usage of the 6,000 kg**

| | Kg |
|---|---|
| 2,800 units of P (× ($0.75/$0.50)) | 4,200 |
| 720 units of M (× ($1.25/$0.50)) | 1,800 |
| | 6,000 |

**Optimum production with additional 1,000 kg**

| | Kg |
|---|---|
| (1,000 – 720) units of M (× ($1.25/$0.50)) | 700 |
| 100 units of N (× ($1.50/$0.50)) | 300 |
| | 1,000 |

Contribution obtainable:

| | $ |
|---|---|
| 280 units of M (× $4.50) | 1,260 |
| 100 units of N (× $4.80) | 480 |
| | 1,740 |

Plus the original purchase price (1,000kgs × $0.5) = $500

Total prepared to pay = **$2,240**

5.3    The correct answers are:

- Marginal costing is appropriate for short-term pricing decisions.
- Absorption costing when used for pricing decisions includes the 'total-cost' of the product.
- Marginal costing is more appropriate than absorption costing for use in one-off pricing decisions.

5.4    The correct answer is: (1,000 × E) + (2,400 × D) + (3,000 × F)

| | D | E | F |
|---|---|---|---|
| Contribution per unit | 54 | 72 | 35 |
| Labour hrs per unit | 1 | 1.5 | 0.5 |
| Contribution per limiting factor | 54/1 = 54 | 72/1.5 = 48 | 35/0.5 = 70 |
| Ranking | 2 | 3 | 1 |

| | Demand | Make | | | | |
|---|---|---|---|---|---|---|
| Product F | 3,000 | 3,000 | 3,000 × 0.5 | = 1,500 | 5,400 – 1,500 | = 3,900 |
| Product D | 2,400 | 2,400 | 2,400 × 1 | = 2,400 | 3,900 – 2,400 | = 1,500 |
| Product E | 2,200 | 1,000* | 1,000 × 1.5 | = 1,500 | | |

*This is a balancing figure. We only have 1,500 labour hours left to use. Product E uses 1.5 hours per unit. So only 1,500/1.5 = 1,000 units can be made.

5.5    The correct answer is: $160.71

Throughput contribution per unit = selling price per unit - material cost per unit

Throughput contribution per unit = $26 – $7.25 = $18.75

BPP
LEARNING MEDIA

Throughput contribution per hour =

$$\$18.72 \times \frac{60}{7} = \$160.71$$

5.6 The correct answer is: $2,000.

First calculate the number of units of inventory left at the end of October.

| Closing inventory units | = | Opening inventory units + units produced − units sold. |
|---|---|---|
| | = | 0 + 4,000 − 3,600 |
| | = | 400 |

Using throughput accounting we include the cost of the materials only:

400 × ( $20,000/4,000 ) = $2,000

5.7 The correct answer is to produce 400 As.

| | A | B | C |
|---|---|---|---|
| | $ | $ | $ |
| Sales price per unit | 20 | 23 | 25 |
| Material cost per unit | 3 | 2 | 4 |
| Labour cost per unit | 5 | 10 | 7.5 |
| Contribution per unit | 12 | 11 | 13.5 |
| Labour hours per unit | 1 | 2 | 1.5 |
| Contribution per labour hour | 12 | 5.5 | 9 |
| Rank | 1 | 3 | 2 |

As demand for each product is unlimited produce 400 As.

5.8 The correct answer is: D.

| | Z1 | Z2 | Z3 |
|---|---|---|---|
| | $ | $ | $ |
| Selling price per unit | 15 | 18 | 17.00 |
| Variable costs per unit | 7 | 11 | 12.70 |
| Contribution per unit | 8 | 7 | 4.30 |
| Labour cost per unit | $2 | $4 | $1.80 |
| Contribution per $1 of labour | $4 | $1.75 | $2.39 |
| Rank order of production | 1 | 3 | 2 |

If you chose option A, you ranked according to contribution per unit.

If you chose option B, you ranked according to variable cost per unit.

If you chose option C, you ranked according to labour cost per unit.

5.9 The correct answer is: Up to but not including $14.50.

The shadow price of a limiting resource is the amount above the normal variable costs that will be added to the total contribution if one extra unit of the scarce resource (here direct labour hours) is made available.

This means that the company would increase contribution by paying up to $10 + $4.50 = $14.50 per hour for additional labour time. However, it would not pay exactly $14.50, as this would leave it no better and no worse off than if it did not have the extra labour hour.

5.10 The correct answers are:

- Subordinate operations to binding constraint
- Identify binding constraint
- Exploit the available capacity

Goldratts steps:

- Identify binding constraint
- Exploit the available capacity

- Subordinate operations to binding constraint
- Elevate the system's bottleneck

Return to Step 1:

Goldratts principles are based around a JIT environment with a buffer stock only allowed in front of the bottleneck machine.

# 6 Relevant costs

6.1 The correct answer is: Adapting now will produce savings of $130,000 more than adapting in one year.

| | | |
|---|---|---|
| Sale of machinery would produce additional income of: | $800,000 – $600,000 | = $200,000 |
| Removal of machinery would save: | $100,000 – $110,000 | = $10,000 |
| Leasing machinery would cost an additional: | $80,000 – $0 | = $80,000 |

A – There will therefore be additional savings of $130,000 ($200,000 + $10,000 – $80,000 = $130,000) by adapting now.

B – If you chose adapting now will cost $130,000 more than in one year, you calculated the correct amount but you got your costs and savings muddled up.

C – If you chose adapting now will produce savings of $110,000 more than adapting in one year, you probably deducted the savings on the removal of machinery instead of adding them.

D – If you chose adapting now will cost $110,000 more than adapting in one year, you probably deducted the savings on the removal of machinery instead of adding them and got the direction of the cash flow the wrong way round.

6.2 The correct answer is: $400,000

Price = variable costs saved of $150,000 + contribution earned on other products of $250,000

= $400,000

6.3 The correct answer is: $376.

| | $ |
|---|---|
| Additional purchases (5 tonnes × $50) | 250 |
| Relevant cost of material M already held: | |
| higher of $126 and (3 × $35) | 126 |
| Relevant cost total | 376 |

If you chose $250 you only took the additional purchases into account and ignored the 3 tonnes in inventory.

If you chose $355 then you costed the 3 tonnes at the realisable value. This is incorrect as the opportunity cost is the higher of the two benefits foregone and in this case more is lost by not being able to use it on the alternative job.

If you chose $400 then you costed all of the material at the replacement cost. This is incorrect as the material is not in regular use.

6.4 The correct answers are:

- Notional costs
- Sunk costs

Avoidable costs and opportunity costs are both relevant as they are incremental and change as a result of a decision.

Notional cost is a hypothetical accounting cost used to reflect the benefit from the use of something for which no actual cash expense is incurred. It is not therefore relevant. Sunk cost is a term used to describe a cost that has already been incurred or committed and which is therefore not relevant to subsequent decisions.

BPP
LEARNING MEDIA

6.5    The correct answer is: Replacement cost.

The relevant cost is the replacement cost of the material because material X is used regularly by the company in its normal business and is available from inventory.

6.6    The correct answer is: $13,600.

The market value is 2 × $8,000 = $16,000. The current resale value is $16,000 × 85% = $13,600. The opportunity cost is the next best alternative foregone and therefore the answer is $13,600.

6.7    The correct answer is: $9,000.

Material Y is at replacement cost of $11 as in regular use. Material X - the 300kg in inventory is at realisable value and that leaves 200kg to buy at replacement cost of $7. Material Z is in inventory and has no other use so would also be costed at realisable value. (300 × $3) + (200 × $7) + (500 × $11) + (100 × $12) = $9,000

If you chose $6,000 then you used historic cost for Y but all other materials were correctly treated.

If you chose $7,600 you forgot about the 200kg of X that was not in inventory but treated everything else correctly.

If you chose $9,300 you used replacement cost for Z, even though it would not be replaced.

6.8    The correct answer is: Net realisable value.

This will, of course, depend on the manner in which they are to be disposed. It might be scrap value less any disposal costs or, if they are sold for an alternative use once work has been carried out on them, the net realisable value will be selling price less the costs of the further work.

Replacement cost is incorrect because replacement cost is not an appropriate relevant cost as the units are no longer required.

Variable cost is incorrect because variable cost is only relevant in certain circumstances (if net realisable value is the same as variable cost).

Full cost is incorrect because full cost includes absorbed fixed overheads, which are not relevant.

6.9    The correct answer is: Book value of the old asset.

All of the other options affect cash flow and are therefore relevant costs.

6.10   The correct answer is: An opportunity cost of $750 and an incremental cost of $1,500.

The relevant cost is an opportunity cost of $750 and an incremental cost of $1,500. If the material is not used on this order 500kg could be sold to generate 1.50 × 500 = $750.

The other 300kg would be purchased at the current price of $5 giving a total of $1,500.

Although the original $2,000 paid for the 500kg in inventory is a sunk cost in this situation there is an alternative use for it. There is not an incremental cost of $4,000 since some of the material required is in inventory.

# 7 Multi-product breakeven analysis

7.1    The correct answers are:

- Total fixed costs/contribution per unit;
- Contribution required to break even/contribution per unit.

Breakeven point is the activity level at which there is neither a profit nor a loss. Alternatively, it is the activity level at which total contribution equals fixed costs.

The contribution to sales ratio gives the proportion of contribution generated by each $ of sales.

Costs to sales ratio is not a recognised ratio.

**7.2** The correct answer is: $250,000.

Profit must increase by $100,000 to make a profit of $250,000.

Contribution to sales ratio is $(1,000 - 600)/1,000$ ie 40%

Therefore sales value needed to make a contribution of $100,000 = $100,000/40% = $250,000

**7.3** The correct answer is: $1,690,000

|  | Superior contract | Standard contact | Basic contract |
|---|---|---|---|
|  | $ | $ | $ |
| Calculate contribution per contract | 550 | 500 | 220 |

Calculate contribution per mix = $0.20 \times \$550 + 0.30 \times \$500 + 0.50 \times \$220 = \$370$

Calculate breakeven point = $\dfrac{\text{Fixed costs}}{\text{Contribution per mix}} = \dfrac{\$1,000,000}{\$370} = 2,703$ mixes

Calculate breakeven in terms of number of contracts

$2,703 \times 0.20 = 541$ units of Superior

$2,703 \times 0.30 = 811$ units of Standard

$2,703 \times 0.50 = 1,352$ units of Basic

Breakeven in terms of revenue

$= 541 \times \$1,000 + 811 \times \$750 + 1,352 \times \$400 = \$1,690,050$

**7.4** The correct answer is: Lower.

The existing contribution to sales (C/S) ratios for each product can be taken straight from the table.

|  | R | S | T |  |
|---|---|---|---|---|
|  | $ | $ | $ |  |
| Calculate contribution per contract | 0.6 | 0.4 | 0.5 | Average C/S ratio = 22,000/45,000 = 0.49 |
| Revised mix |  |  |  |  |
| Sales (W1) | 9,000 | 22,500 | 13,500 | 45,000 |
| Contribution (W2) | 5,400 | 9,000 | 6,750 | 21,150 |
| Average C/S ratio (W3) |  |  |  | 0.47 |

Workings

1 The new sales revenue mix will affect the sales of each product. Thus for product R, the new sales figure will be $0.20 \times \$45,000 = \$9,000$ and so on for the other two products.

2 Contribution is worked out by taking the current contribution to sales ratio (C/S ratio) and applying this to the new sales figure for each product. Taking product R again, the current C/S ratio is 60%, so multiply the new sales figure by 60% which gives $5,400 and so on for all three products.

3 This is worked out as $(21,150/45,000)$.

This is a long-hand way of doing the calculation but easier to understand if you prefer working from first principles. The examiner just multiplies through the existing C/S ratios by the new ratios thus:

$(0.6 \times 0.2) + (0.4 \times 0.5) + (0.5 \times 0.3) = 0.47$

**7.5** The correct answer is: 47.6%

|  | Basic | Standard | Advanced | Total |
|---|---|---|---|---|
| **Revenue per mix** |  |  |  |  |
| Selling price ($) | 50 | 100 | 135 |  |
| Contracts sold | 750 | 450 | 300 |  |
| Total ($) | 37,500 | 45,000 | 40,500 | 123,000 |
| **Contribution per mix** |  |  |  |  |
| Contribution ($) | 20 | 50 | 70 |  |
| Contracts sold | 750 | 450 | 300 |  |
| Total | 15,000 | 22,500 | 21,000 | 58,500 |

Average C/S ratio = 58,500/123,000 = 47.6%

BPP LEARNING MEDIA

7.6    The correct answer is: $125,000.

Breakeven point in units = Fixed costs/contribution per unit

= $50,000 / ($25 × 0.4)

= 5,000.

Breakeven sales revenue = 5,000 × $25

= $125,000

Alternatively, sales revenue at breakeven point = Fixed costs / C/S ratio

= $50,000 / 0.4

= $125,000

7.7    The correct answer is: $2,312,500.

Sales revenue to breakeven = Fixed costs/ C/S ratio

Therefore $2m = $800,000/C/S ratio

Therefore C/S ratio = $800,000/$2m = 0.4

Total contribution for targeted profit = Fixed costs + required profit

= $800,000 + $125,000

= $925,000

To convert this target contribution into sales revenue we use the C/S ratio.

$925,000/0.4 = $2,312,500

7.8    The correct answer is: $7,143,000.

At the breakeven point, sales revenue = fixed costs/C/S ratio.

From the question, fixed costs = $25 per consulting hour × 100,000 hours. The C/S ratio is given and is 35%.

So sales revenue = ($25 × 100,000)/0.35 = $7,142,857 which is closest to $7,143,000.

If you chose $875,000 then you multiplied the fixed costs by the C/S ratio and didn't divide which was the correct treatment.

If you chose $1,786,000 then you only took the 25,000 per quarter and did not multiply this by 4 to give annual overheads. You then correctly divided by 0.35. If you got $219,000 you made the same mistake but then compounded it by multiplying by 0.35.

7.9    The correct answers are:

Point A        Break even point if services sold in the order K, L, N, M.
Point B        Multi product breakeven point

**Point A**: is the company's **breakeven point** on the **assumption that the services are sold in order of their C/S ratio**, all of the service with the highest C/S ratio (service K 0.56) being sold first, all of the service with the second highest C/S ratio (service L 0.38) second, then N (0.35) and then finally M, which actually has a negative C/S ratio. We base the ratio on gross contribution (ie before any fixed costs).

**Point B**: is the **average breakeven point** for RDF Co on the **assumption that the services are sold in the ratio 1,000: 2,300: 1,450, 1,970** until the breakeven sales value is reached.

7.10   The correct answer is: $1,692.

$$\text{Average C/S ratio} = \frac{(3 \times 27\%) + (2 \times 56\%) + (5 \times 38\%)}{(3 + 2 + 5)} = 38.3\%$$

At breakeven point, contribution = fixed costs

$$\therefore \frac{\$648,000}{\text{Breakeven sales revenue}} = 0.383$$

∴ Breakeven sales revenue = $1,691,906

Therefore the answer is $1,692.

7.11    The correct answer is:  53%

Contribution = $500,000 – 90,000 – 80,000 – 30,000 = 300,000
Per unit = $300,000/600,000 units = $0.50

Reduction in sales volume = 160,000/$0.50 = 280,000 units

Margin of safety: (600,000 -280,000)/600,000 = 53.3%

7.12    The correct answer is: $620,000

Breakeven sales revenue = fixed costs/weighted average c/s ratio

Contribution Y: 61-42 = 19
Contribution Z: 95-63 = 32
Total contribution for mix = (19 × 4) + (32 × 2) = 140
Total sales = (61 × 4) + (95 × 2) = 434
C/S ratio = 140/434 = 0.3226

Breakeven revenue = $200,000/0.3226 = $619,963 or $620,000 rounded up

7.13    The correct answer is: The contribution earned by Product B grows more quickly than the contribution earned
by product A as sales levels increase

70% of the selling price of product A contributes to fixed overheads and profits, but for product B it is 74%.

If both products were made in the same department then product B would have a lower break-even point than
product A, however the fixed overheads in department making B could be much higher than in A meaning that
this statement is not true.

Variable costs are four percentage points higher for product A compared to B, but this is not the same as
being 4% higher.

# 8 Short-term decision making

8.1     The correct answer is: $7,776.

|  | $ |
| --- | --- |
| N revenue ($32.40 × (8,100 × 0.9)) | 236,196 |
| Further processing costs (8,100 × $16.20) | (131,220) |
| Share of joint costs $210,600 × (8,100 / 17,550) | (97,200) |
| Profit | 7,776 |

8.2     The correct answer is: If those units bought from the subcontractor have the lowest extra variable cost per
unit of scarce resource saved.

For example, if machine hours are a scarce resource, a company should minimise the extra variable cost of
subcontracting per machine hour saved.

8.3     The correct answer is: Costs used for decision making never include fixed costs.

It is not true to say that costs used for decision making never include fixed costs. Fixed costs that arise as a
direct result of the decision are relevant costs. They would therefore be included in costs used for decision
making and for costs used for profit reporting.

8.4     The correct answer is: Division W and Division X only

|  | W | X | Y |
| --- | --- | --- | --- |
|  | $'000 | $'000 | $'000 |
| Contribution | 140 | 420 | 60 |
| Fixed overheads* | 70 | 70 | 70 |
| Profit | 70 | 350 | -10 |

*Fixed overheads specific to divisions = ($525,000 × 40%) / 3 = $70,000 per division

8.5    The correct answer is: Variance analysis.

Feedforward control is based on comparing original targets or actual results with a forecast of future results.

8.6    The correct answer is: $69,522.

**Top tips**. Note that as a first step, we need to deduct the proceeds of $18,000 for by product Z from the joint production costs of $140,000. This will give us the net joint production costs of $122,000. These will be apportioned to products X and Y on the basis of the final sales value of these products. As a third step, after the apportionment on the basis of sales value, we add the further processing costs to arrive at the total production costs for X.

|  | $ |
|---|---|
| Joint production costs for W, Y, Z | 140,000 |
| Less: Proceeds from by product Z: | |
| $6 × 3,000 | (18,000) |
| Net joint costs to be apportioned | 122,000 |

Sales revenue from X and Y:

|  | $ |
|---|---|
| X (2,500 units × $50) | 125,000 |
| Y (3,500 units × $60) | 210,000 |
|  | 335,000 |

Apportioning net joint costs on the basis of sales revenue:

$$X: \left( \frac{\$125,000}{\$335,000} \times \$122,000 \right) + \$24,000 = \$69,522$$

**Top tips**. The question is only asking for the total cost of producing X. The cost of producing Y is worked out below but it would not be necessary in the exam.

$$Y: \left( \frac{\$210,000}{\$335,000} \times 122,000 \right) + \$46,000 = \$122,475$$

8.7    The correct answer is:  $80,000

If component B is purchased the contribution earned will be $45,000 and the variable cost saved will be $35,000. So the maximum that HM Co would be willing to pay = $45,000 + $35,000 = $80,000

8.8    The correct answer is: $4,500

|  | $ |
|---|---|
| 900kg in inventory could be sold for $3.50 = | 3,150 |
| Remainder will be bought 300kg × $4.50 | 1,350 |
| Relevant cost | 4,500 |

8.9    The correct answer is: Component Y only

|  | X | Y | Z |
|---|---|---|---|
|  | $ | $ | $ |
| Subcontractor price | 8 | 14 | 11 |
| Variable cost | 5 | 16 | 10 |
| Difference | 3 | −2 | 1 |

Component Y is cheaper to buy from the supplier than to make.

8.10   The correct answers are:

- Incremental costs
- Differential costs
- Opportunity costs

8.11 The correct answer is: 1,000 As, 2,000 Bs and 500 Cs

|  | A | B | C |
|---|---|---|---|
|  | $ | $ | $ |
| Selling price | 50 | 68 | 94 |
| Material A | (20) | (30) | (40) |
| Material B | (5) | (8) | (10) |
| Labour | (10) | (5) | (15) |
| Contribution per unit | 15 | 25 | 29 |
| Kgs of Mat A per unit | 2 | 3 | 4 |
| Contribution per kg A | 7.5 | 8.33 | 7.25 |
| Rank | 2 | 1 | 3 |

Optimal production plan:

|  |  | kgs |
|---|---|---|
| Available |  | 10,000 |
| Make max number of Bs | (2,000 × 3) | (6,000) |
| Make max number of As | (1,000 × 2) | (2,000) |
|  |  | 2,000 |
| Use rest to make Cs @ 4kgs | 2,000/4 = 500 | (2,000) |

8.12 The correct answer is: $420,000

|  | K | P |
|---|---|---|
|  | $ | $ |
| Selling price | 160 | 98 |
| Mat C | 20 | 0 |
| Mat D | 20 | 20 |
| Labour | 60 | 40 |
| Contribution | 60 | 38 |
| Labour hours | 3 | 2 |
| Contribution per hour | 20 | 19 |
| Rank | 1 | 2 |

Optimal production plan:

We are not told that there is a maximum demand for either product, therefore assume the 21,000 hours are used to manufacture Ks @$20 per hour = $420,000

# 9 Linear programming

9.1 The correct answer is: $3J + 2T \leq 3,300$.

Let Jackets = J and Trousers = T.

The total available is 4,000m. However, 700m is required for the contract ($200 \times 3 + 50 \times 2$) and therefore the amount to be considered in the decision is reduced to 3300. The correct answer is therefore $3J + 2T \leq 3,300$.

If you chose $3J + 2T \leq 4,000$ you did not deduct the amount required for the special contract. If you chose $3T + 2J \leq 4,700$ you added the amount required for the special contract on to the total requirement incorrectly instead of deducting it and you mixed up J and T.

If you chose $3T + 2J \leq 3,300$ you mixed up T and J in your resource requirements.

9.2 The correct answers are:

- The contribution that can be earned from one additional unit of scarce resource.
- The premium that should be paid for one additional unit of scarce resource.
- The premium that should be paid for additional resources where there is no slack of that resource.

BPP LEARNING MEDIA

The following are not correct because:

- A shadow price is not the minimum that should be paid for scarce resource as this would mean that the amount paid would always exceed contribution that could be earned from it.

- It is also not the total that should be paid. The shadow price needs to be added to the normal price per unit to determine the total that should be paid.

- The other options are all ways of defining a shadow price.

9.3 The correct answer is: There is slack material.

This can be calculated as:

$500 \times 3 + 200 \times 7 + 100 \times 2 = 3,100$. This means there are 400 units of slack material.

There is no slack labour as $500 \times 2 + 200 \times 1 + 100 \times 4 = 1,600$. This is the total availability.

9.4 The correct answer is: C = 45T + 35S

Contribution per unit of T = $130 − $25 − $40 − $20 = $45

Contribution per unit of S = $145 − $30 − $50 − $30 = $35

If you chose C = 45S + 35T, you got T and S the wrong way round. If you chose C = 35T + 30S, you incorrectly included the fixed overhead cost. If you chose C = 30S + 35T you incorrectly included the fixed overhead cost and you mixed up T and S.

9.5 The correct order is:

| | |
|---|---|
| Define the variables | 1st |
| Plot a graph | 3rd |
| Identify feasible area | 4th |
| Plot Iso contribution line | 5th |
| Formulate constraints and objective function | 2nd |
| Determine optimal solution | 6th |

9.6 The correct answers are:

- Total amount of scarce resource is known with certainty.
- Fixed costs are unchanged by the decision.
- There is no interdependence of demand between product.
- Unit variable cost is constant.

All are assumptions apart from the statement that says we assume units of output are not divisible. We have to assume that units are divisible. This is necessary to calculate optimal solutions and shadow prices. We also assume that there is no interdependence between products.

9.7 The correct answer is: $1.5J + 0.75T \leq 1,662.5$.

Let Jackets = J and Trousers = T

The total available is 2,000m. However, 337.5m is required for the contract ($200 \times 1.5 + 50 \times 0.75$) and therefore the amount to be considered in the decision is reduced to 1,662.50. The correct answer is therefore $1.5J + 0.75T \leq 1,662.5$.

If you chose $1.5J + 0.75T \leq 2,000$ you did not deduct the amount required for the special contract. If you chose $1.5J + 0.75T \leq 2,337.5$ you added the amount required for the special contract on to the total requirement incorrectly instead of deducting it.

If you chose $0.75J + 1.5T \leq 1,662.5$ you mixed up T and J in your resource requirements.

9.8 The correct answers are:

- X = 700
- Y = 400

| 1 | 6x + 4y | = 5,800 |
| 2 | 14x − 10y | = 5,800 |

Multiply (1) by 10 and (2) by 4

| 3 | 60x + 40y | = 58,000 |
| 4 | 56x − 40y | = 23,200 |

(3) + (4) = 116x = 81,200

X = 700

Substitute in (1):

| 6x + 4y | = 5,800 |
| 4,200 + 4y | = 5,800 |
| 4y | = 1,600 |
| Y | = 400 |

9.9 The correct answer is: $32.50.

The shadow price for material X is the contribution that can be generated per m.

This is the unit contribution of $65 divided by the number of metres (2) = $32.50

9.10 The correct answer is: $N - H < 0$

This can be seen if we substitute in 10 healthy items and 9 non healthy. The directive here is being followed.

9 − 10 = -1. This is less than 0.

9.11 The correct answers are:

- Identify the feasible area
- Formulate the constraints

Aside from these, linear programming requires a graph to be plotted, with an iso contribution line and the constraints and objective function formulated.

Allocating costs to cost pools and identifying cost drivers relate to Activity Based Costing (ABC), whilst identifying the breakeven point is a step in Cost Volume Profit (CVP) analysis.

9.12 The correct answer is: 2,250.

Workings

4W + 2T = 12,500 (1)

3W + 4T = 15,000 (2)

Multiply equation (1) by two so we can eliminate T:

8W + 4T = 25,000 (3)

Subtract equation (2) from equation (3)

8W + 4T = 25,000 less

3W + 4T = 15,000

5W = 10,000

W = 2,000

Substitute W = 2,000 into equation (1)

BPP LEARNING MEDIA

$4 \times 2{,}000 + 2T = 12{,}500$

$8{,}000 + 2T = 12{,}500$

$2T = 12{,}500 - 8{,}000$

$T = 2{,}250$

9.13    The correct answer is: $C = 17K + 15A$.

The iso-contribution line will represent the contribution (selling price less variable costs) that each product makes. The K makes $17 per unit, and the A $15 per unit. If you arrived at the figures of $7 and $6 you were incorrectly taking account of fixed overheads to calculate profit, not contribution.

# 10 Forecasting techniques

10.1    The correct answer is: A peak in the first three years of every decade, with a corresponding trough in the last five years of every decade.

Regular cycles involving an increase in the first half of each year, followed by a corresponding decrease in the second half of the year is an example of seasonal variations, which are short-term fluctuations in recorded values.

An increase of the same amount each year is an increasing trend.

A peak in the first three years of every decade with a corresponding trough in the last five years of the decade is an example of a cyclical variation, which is a medium term change in results caused by circumstances which repeat in cycles.

Occasional peaks which occur unpredictably but on average once every five years is an example of random variations, which are unpredictable.

10.2    The correct answer is: $12,120

Direct material cost per 1% activity = $40

Direct labour cost per 1% activity is not a constant amount at both activity levels, so this must be a semi-variable cost. Since production overhead is also a semi-variable cost the two costs can be analysed together, to save time (since the question asks only for a total cost in the answer).

|  | $ |
| --- | --- |
| Direct labour and production overhead |  |
| At 80% activity | 8,200 |
| At 90% activity | 8,700 |
| Change 10% | 500 |

Variable cost per 1% change in activity = $\dfrac{\$500}{10\%}$ = $50

Substituting in 80% activity:

|  | $ |
| --- | --- |
| Variable cost = 80 × $50 | 4,000 |
| Total cost | 8,200 |
| ∴ Fixed cost | 4,200 |

Flexed budget cost at 88% level of activity

|  |  | $ |
| --- | --- | --- |
| Direct material (88 × $40) |  | 3,520 |
| Direct labour and production overhead: | Variable (88 × $50) | 4,400 |
| Fixed |  | 4,200 |
|  |  | 12,120 |

10.4 The correct answers are:
- a is a constant, a fixed amount;
- x is the independent variable, whose value helps to determine the corresponding value of y;
- y is the dependent variable, depending for its value on the value of x

10.5 The correct answer is: 326 units.

The trend must be 'moved on' from quarter 8 to 11. ie

$330.625 + (3 \times 6) = 348.625$, and to this must be added the average seasonal variation of $-22.5$ ie $348.625 - 22.5 = 326.125$ units.

10.6 The correct answer is: An underlying long-term movement over time in the values of the data recorded.

A short-term fluctuation due to different circumstances which affect results at different points in time is a seasonal variation.

A medium-term change in results caused by circumstances which repeat in cycles is a cyclical variation.

A non-recurring fluctuation caused by unforeseen circumstances is a random variation.

10.7 The correct answer is: $1,739,000

The trend for year 8 quarter 4 is $1,632,000 and the trend is to increase by $25,000 per quarter.

The trend for year 10 quarter 1 is therefore $1,632,000 + (5 \times $25,000) = $1,757,000.

The seasonal variation for quarter 1 is $-$18,000 and so the sales forecast for year 10 quarter 1 is $1,757,000 $-$ $18,000 = $1,739,000.

10.8 The correct answer is: At the mid-point of the period to which they apply.

A moving average is an average of the results of a fixed number of periods.

10.9 The correct answer is: $114,400

From the regression equation, variable cost per unit is $286. If production is 400 units, variable production cost is

$286 $\times$ 400 = $114,400.

10.10 The correct answer is: $17,600

| | | | Difference |
|---|---|---|---|
| Output | 2,000 units | 3,500 units | 1,500 units |
| Total cost | $12,000 | $16,200 | $4,200 |

Variable cost per unit = $\dfrac{\$4,200}{1,500}$ = $2.80

Fixed cost = 12,000 $-$ (2,000 $\times$ $2.80) = $6,400

The budgeted cost allowance for 4,000 units = $6,400 + (4,000 $\times$ $2.80) = $17,600

10.11 The correct answer is: $794,520

| Month | | Labour hours | Cost |
|---|---|---|---|
| January | | 15,000 | $18,000 + (3 \times 15,000) = $63,000 |
| February | (15,000 $\times$ 1.04) | 15,600 | $18,000 + (3 \times 15,600) = $64,800 |
| March – December | (15,600 $\times$ 1.04) | 16,224 | 10 $\times$ [$18,000 + (3 \times 16,224)] = $666,720 |
| Total | | | $794,520 |

10.12 The correct answer is: $3,990

$2,750/250 = $11 per unit including index, adjusting to the base year ($11/1.1) gives a base year cost of $10 per unit.

In month 3 the index is 114, therefore the unit cost is 10 $\times$ 1.14 =$11.40

For 350 units prediction: 350 $\times$ $11.40 = $3,990

BPP LEARNING MEDIA

10.13 The correct answer is: Prediction of future costs for activity levels within the company's relevant range

Regression analysis can be used to predict future costs, but only within the company's relevant range (ie the range for which it has experience of past costs) as extrapolation beyond this level could be unreliable. For example, beyond this range may result in extra fixed costs.

Using regression analysis does not identify the cause of costs or explain deviations from budgeted costs.

# 11a Budgeting for planning

11a.1 The correct answer is: Budgetary planning

Strategic (or corporate) planning covers periods longer than one year. Operation planning is planning on a very short-term or day-to-day basis. Budgetary or tactical planning involves preparing detailed plans which generally cover one year.

11a.2 The correct answers are:

- Purchasing budget
- Sales budget
- Marketing cost budget

All are functional budgets except for a cash budget. A functional budget is a budget of income and/or expenditure for a particular department or process. A cash budget does not relate to a function.

11a.3 The correct answer is: $60,532

| | $ |
|---|---|
| 40% of May sales for cash (40% × $55,000) | 22,000 |
| 70% of April credit sales less 2% discount (70% × 60% × $70,000 × 98%) | 28,812 |
| 27% of March credit sales (27% × 60% × $60,000) | 9,720 |
| | 60,532 |

11a.4 The correct answer is:

Zero-based budgeting is a method of budgeting whereby all activities are re-evaluated each time a budget is formatted.

'A method of budgeting that recognises the difference between the behaviour of fixed and variable costs with respect to changes in output and the budget is designed to change appropriately with such fluctuations' describes a flexible budget.

The other two answers are incorrect and do not describe any type of budget.

11a.5 The correct answers are:

| | | |
|---|---|---|
| A | Take action to adjust the capacity of resources to match the projected supply | 4th |
| B | Determine the resources that are required to perform organisation activities | 3rd |
| C | Estimate the production and sales volume by individual products and customers | 1st |
| D | Estimate the demand for organisational activities | 2nd |

## 11a.6 The correct answer is: $86

| | July $ | August $ | September $ | October $ |
|---|---|---|---|---|
| Sales | 100 | 90 | 125 | 140 |
| Opening inventory | | | | |
| (Sales × 50%) / 125% | (40) | (36) | (50) | (56) |
| Required for this month's sales (Sales/125%) | 80 | 72 | 100 | |
| Closing inventory (see opening inventory in next month) | 36 | 50 | 56 | |
| Purchases | 76 | 86 | 106 | |
| Paid | | 76 | 86 | 106 |

## 11a.7 The correct answer is: Both 1 and 2

By producing new plans at regular intervals, such as every three months, there may be a tendency for management to focus in changes to the plan rather than aspects of performance that should be controlled. They are time-consuming, and are only worthwhile when there is continual and substantial uncertainty about the future. (A simpler alternative if needed is to amend the annual budget when the budget is clearly unrealistic or out-of-date, by preparing an updated annual budget.)

## 11a.8 The correct answer is: Management budgets may not be realistic in practice.

When senior managers impose budgets on managers below them in the organisation hierarchy, there is a risk that the imposed budgets will be unrealistic because senior managers may not have a full understanding of operational realities.

## 11a.9 The correct answers are:

Difficulty in quantifying objectives

Difficulty in quantifying outputs

In private sector companies, objectives and outputs are fairly easy to identify, at least in the short term, as sales and profits. In the public sector, there are multiple non-financial objectives and many different ways of measuring output which creates complexity in the process. Budgeting within a spending limit should not necessarily make budgeting a difficult task.

## 11a.10 The correct answer is: $109,200

| | Month of credit Sale | | | Received |
|---|---|---|---|---|
| | September | October | November | December |
| Factor × $100,000 | 15% | – | – | 15,000 |
| Factor × $120,000 | – | 20% | – | 24,000 |
| Factor × $130,000 | – | – | 60% × 90% | 70,200 |
| | | | | 109,200 |

## 11a.11 The correct answer is: $18,450

| | | Litres |
|---|---|---|
| Litres required for sales | (5,546 × 2) | 11,092 |
| Total required for production | (11,092/0.94) | 11,800 |
| Plus increase in closing inventory | | 500 |
| Required purchases | | 12,300 |

12,300 litres @ $1.50 each = $18,450

## 11a.12 The correct answer is: $660,000

| | | Hours |
|---|---|---|
| Labour hours required for production | (11,875 × 4) | 47,500 |
| Total time, including Idle time (5% of total hours required) | 47,500/0.95 | 50,000 |

BPP LEARNING MEDIA

40,000 @ $12 = $480,000
10,000 @ $18 = $180,000
Total          $660,000

11a.13 The correct answer is: $15,615

|          |                          | $      |
|----------|--------------------------|--------|
| April    | (0.2 × 18,000)           | 3,600  |
| March    | (0.5 × 17,000 × 0.99)    | 8,415  |
| February | (0.15 × 16,000)          | 2,400  |
| January  | (0.1 × 12,000)           | 1,200  |
| Total    |                          | 15,615 |

Bad debts are ignored as they do not correspond to a cash inflow.

11a.14 The correct answers are:

Does not affect the optimal solution in a linear programming solution – a non-binding constraint.

Is altered to reflect the actual level of activity – a flexed budget

Constrains what the business can achieve in the budget period – a bottleneck resource

# 11b Budgeting for performance evaluation and control

11b.1 The correct answer is: $163,250

Use the high low method to calculate the total fixed costs and the variable costs per unit.

|                          | Units  | $       |
|--------------------------|--------|---------|
| Highest level of activity | 15,000 | 177,500 |
| Lowest level of activity  | 10,000 | 130,000 |
| Difference                | 5,000  | 47,500  |

The variable costs = 47,500/5000 = $9.50

Substitute this value into one of the total cost equations to find the total fixed cost:

Total cost – (variable cost per unit × number of units) = fixed cost

177,500 – (9.50 × 15,000 ) = 35,000

Therefore total cost equation is: y = 35,000 + 9.5 x

When x = 13,500, y = 35,000 + (9.5 × 13,500) = $163,250

11b.2 The correct answer is: The budgeted cost expected for the actual level of activity achieved during the period.

A budget cost allowance is the expected expenditure in a budget which has been flexed to the actual level of activity. It includes a basic, unchanged allowance for fixed costs and an amount for variable costs according to the level of activity.

A budget of expenditure applicable to a particular function describes a functional budget and a budget set without permitting the ultimate budget manager the opportunity to participate in budget setting is an imposed or top-down budget. A budget cost allowance includes an amount for variable overhead and so a fixed budget for expenditure which is expected every period regardless of the level of activity is not correct.

**11b.3** The correct answer is: $237,500

Direct material costs = $60,000/5,000 × 8,000 = $96,000

Production labour (high-low method):

| Units | Labour |
|---|---|
| | $ |
| 7,000 | 65,000 |
| 5,000 | 52,000 |
| 2,000 | 13,000 |

Variable cost per unit = $13,000/2,000 = $6.50

Fixed cost element:

$65,000 = FC + (7,000 × $6.5)

FC = $65,000 - $45,500 = $19,500

Labour cost in quarter 3 = $19,500 + (8,000 × $6.5) = $71,500

Production overheads are fixed at $70,000

Total cost = $96,000 + $71,500 + $70,000 = $237,500

**11b.4** The correct answers are: Model 1 and Model 3.

A feedforward control system involves forecasting future outcomes, and comparing these with desired outcomes. Control action is then taken to minimise or remove any differences. These two models are therefore feedforward control models. The inventory control model is a feedback control model, because it provides information on what has already happened, for comparison with a standard or plan (which in this case is the maximum or minimum inventory level).

**11b.5** The correct answer is: $81,000

The variable cost per unit = ($93,000 − $15,000)/13,000 = 6

Fixed element for activity up to 9,999 units = $58,000 − (8,000 × $6) = $10,000.

11,000 units = $15,000 + (11,000 × $6) = $81,000.

**11b.6** The correct answer is: Both 1 and 2

Flexible budgets enable actual results to be compared with expected results for the same volume of activity, such as production and sales. To reconcile an original budgeted profit to actual profit with variances there must be a sales volume variance (measured in terms of either budgeted/standard contribution or profit, depending on the type of costing system used).

**11b.7** The correct answer is: $264,000

| | Production costs | Selling costs |
|---|---|---|
| | $'000 | $'000 |
| Cost of 7,000 units | 231 | 19 |
| Cost of 5,000 units | 195 | 15 |
| Variable cost of 2,000 units | 36 | 4 |
| Variable cost per unit | $18 | $2 |
| | | |
| | $'000 | $'000 |
| Total cost of 5,000 units | 195 | 15 |
| Variable cost of 5,000 units | 90 | 10 |
| Fixed costs | 105 | 5 |
| | | |
| | | $'000 |
| Variable cost of selling 6,000 units (× $18) | | 108 |
| Variable cost of selling 5,500 units (× $2) | | 11 |
| Fixed costs (105 + 35 + 5) | | 145 |
| Total budgeted cost allowance | | 264 |

BPP LEARNING MEDIA

**11b.8** The correct answers are:

- It is the measurement of differences between planned outputs and forecast outputs
- It is a proactive technique as it anticipates problems before they actually occur

Variance analysis is not an example of feedforward control because variance calculations are performed at the end of the period, which makes them an example of feedback control.

**11b.9** The correct answer is: $31,500

Use the high/low method:

|  | Volume | $ |
|---|---|---|
| Highest activity level | 6,500 | 33,000 |
| Lowest activity level | 4,500 | 29,000 |
|  | 2,000 | 4,000 |

∴ Variable cost of 2,000 units is $4,000

∴ Variable cost per unit $\frac{\$4,200}{2,000}$ = $2

∴ Variable cost of 4,500 units = 4,500 × $2
= $9,000

∴ Fixed cost = total cost - variable cost (of 4,500)
= $(29,000 - 9,000)= $20,000

∴ Budget cost for 5,750 units = fixed cost + variable cost of 5,750 units
= $20,000 + (5,750 × $2)
= $31,500

**11b.10** The correct answer is: 33.3%

|  | Original | Revised |
|---|---|---|
|  | $ | $ |
| Revenue | 100 | 60 |
| Variable costs | 30 | 18 |
| Fixed costs | 22 | 22 |
| Profit | 48 | 20 |

The revised profit of $20 is 1/3 of the revised revenue of $60.

If you chose 20% then you calculated 20 as a percentage of the original revenue of $100 not the revised $60.

If you chose 60% you assumed that the profit would follow the pattern of the reduction in revenue. This is not the case.

# 12 Standard costing and variance analysis

**12.1** The correct answer is: Standard costing is useful where products are non standard or are customised to a customer's specifications.

Standard costs work well when homogenous items are being produced, because the company can have an expected usage of inputs for each product, which can be used to value each item of inventory. This simplifies the bookkeeping as well as having the benefit of being useful as a future cost prediction tool. Variance analysis can be used to understand if the standard costs were achieved during a control period.

**12.2** The correct answers are:

- Hiring of more highly skilled workforce.
- Higher quality material purchased.
- Workforce motivated to perform well with higher bonuses for efficiency.

The more highly skilled workforce is likely to operate more efficiently than the standard workforce, thus resulting in a favourable efficiency variance.

The purchase of higher quality material might result in less wastage of material and therefore less wastage of time in the production process which would give a favourable labour efficiency variance.

A workforce motivated to perform well with higher bonuses for efficiency will improve efficiency levels.

Out of date machinery resulting in delays in the production process would mean that labour would be less efficient, which would generate an adverse labour efficiency variance.

Over absorption of overheads does not explain a favourable variance for efficiency.

12.3 The correct answer is: Current standard.

- Budgeted capacity is associated with current standards.
- Budgeted capacity is not associated with basic standards.
- Practical capacity is associated with attainable standards.
- Full capacity is associated with ideal standards.

12.4 The correct answer is: The quantity of work achievable at standard performance in an hour.

For example if the standard time allowance per unit is 4 hours and 22 units are produced, output expressed in terms of standard hours will be 88 standard hours.

An hour during which only standard units are made is not correct. Many organisations make only standard units all the time. A standard hour is a measure of output based on standard levels of performance.

An hour during which no machine breakdowns occur is not correct. Hours free from breakdowns may be what an organisation aims for, but a standard hour is a measure of output based on standard levels of performance.

An hour for which standard labour rates are paid is not correct. This would result in a zero labour rate variance.

12.5 The correct answer is: $166 adverse.

The standard data can be used to determine the standard price per litre for each material:

W = $1,400 / 700 litres
  = $2 per litre
P = $600 / 400 litres
  = $1.50 per litre

The next problem is whether the calculation of the price variance should be based on materials used or materials purchased. Since stocks are valued at standard price, all of the price variance is eliminated immediately the stocks are received, so the variance should be based on purchases.

|  | Should cost | Did cost | Price variance |
|---|---|---|---|
|  | $ | $ | $ |
| 670 litres of W (× $2) | 1,340 | 1,474 | 134 (A) |
| 320 litres of P (× $1.5) | 480 | 512 | 32 (A) |
|  | 1,820 | 1,986 | 166 (A) |

12.6 The correct answer is: It is difficult to identify a standard item for costing.

With road haulage and distribution, drivers' times on the road are measured automatically. Variable costs can be high (labour and fuel for example). Standard costing is more common in manufacturing, but the principle can be applied to service industries.

The problem is to identify a standard item for which cost can be measured and variances subsequently calculated. In road haulage the standard would need to take into account distance travelled, size and weight and any special circumstances (eg refrigeration) which make it hard to establish a standard.

BPP LEARNING MEDIA

12.7   The correct answer is: $7,440 A

|                              | Units    |
|------------------------------|----------|
| Budgeted sales (should sell) | 1,200    |
| Actual sales (did sell)      | 1,080    |
| Difference                   | 120      |
| Valued at standard contribution | $7,440 A |

Standard contribution per unit: 0.31 × $200 = $62

12.8   The correct answers are:

- An increase in the quantity of material purchased helped buyers to earn unexpected bulk discounts.
- The material purchased was of a lower quality than standard.

The unit price of material would be reduced as a result of the bulk discount and buying lower quality material.

The unit price of material would not be reduced by reducing the quantity purchased or improving the processing methods.

12.9   The correct answer is: Basic standard.

- An ideal standard is a standard which can be attained under perfect operating conditions.
- An attainable standard is a standard which can be achieved if production occurs efficiently. Some allowance is made for wastage and inefficiencies.
- A current standard is based on current working conditions.

12.10   The correct answer is: Neither 1 nor 2 are correct.

There is likely to be a demotivating effect where an ideal standard of performance is set, because adverse efficiency variances will always be reported. It is important that adverse variances are not used to lay blame if targets have been set with the aim of motivation.

A low standard of efficiency is also demotivating, because there is no sense of achievement in attaining the required standards. Managers and employees will often outperform the standard or target when in fact they could have performed even better if they had been sufficiently motivated.

12.11   The correct answer is: 14,000 hours

$6,000 variance @ $3 per hour = 2,000 labour hours.

Actual hours worked were 12,000 meaning that 14,000 hours must have been paid.

12.12   The correct answer is: $4.50

Standard cost of material purchased – Actual cost of material purchased = Price variance

Standard cost   = $32,195 – $1,370
                = $30,825

Standard price per kg = $\dfrac{\$30,825}{6,850}$

                = $4.50

12.13   The correct answer is: $14

|                                         | $       |
|-----------------------------------------|---------|
| 300 labour hours should have cost (× $c) | ?       |
| But did cost                            | 4,800   |
|                                         | 600 (A) |

So 300 labour hours should have cost: $4,800 – $600 = $4,200

$4,200/300 = $14 per hour

**12.14** The correct answer is: Both 1 and 2

Statement (1) is consistent with a favourable materials price variance. In a period of inflation, and with a **mid-year standard price**, reported variances early in the year would probably be favourable.

Statement (2) is consistent with a favourable materials price variance. Bulk purchase discounts may **reduce the unit price paid for materials.**

**12.15** The correct answer is: Both 1 and 2

The direct material price variance is $2,000 adverse ($800 adverse – $1,200 favourable).

Both statements are consistent with the variances, because both situations would lead to a **higher price** for materials (adverse material price variance) and **lower usage** (favourable material usage variance).

**12.16** The correct answer is:

| Capacity | Efficiency |
|----------|------------|
| Adverse | Favourable |

The standard time per unit was budgeted at 1.45 hours (82,650/57,000). Actual production should therefore have taken 60,000 × 1.45 = 87,000, but did take 80,000 hours meaning it was favourable.

The original plan was to work 82,650 units, but only 80,000 hours were worked, meaning that the factory operated below capacity.

---

# 13 Further variance analysis

**13.1** The correct answer is: $30,000 adverse.

| | | $ |
|---|---|---|
| Materials price planning variance | | |
| Original standard cost of revised standard usage for actual output: | | |
| ($4.00 × 3 kg × 10,000) | = | 120,000 |
| Revised standard cost of revised standard usage for actual output | | |
| ($5.00 × 3kg × 10,000) | = | 150,000 |
| | | 30,000 A |

**13.2** The correct answer is: $10,000 adverse.

| | kg |
|---|---|
| Materials operational usage variance | |
| 10,000 units should use 3 kg per unit | 30,000 |
| 10,000 units did use | 32,000 |
| | 2,000 A |

2,000 kg at standard revised cost of $5 per kg = $10,000 adverse

**13.3** The correct answer is: $5,000 favourable

Standard mix: $\frac{3}{5}$ G, $\frac{2}{5}$ H

| Material | Actual input Litres | Standard mix of actual input* Litres | Variance Litres | × standard price $ | Variance $ |
|----------|------|------|------|------|------|
| G | 24,500 | 27,000 | 2,500 (F) | 4 | 10,000 (F) |
| H | 20,500 | 18,000 | 2,500 (A) | 2 | 5,000 (A) |
| | 45,000 | 45,000 | – | | 5,000 (F) |

*45,000 × (9/15) = 27,000 litres
45,000 × (6/15) = 18,000 litres

BPP LEARNING MEDIA

**Alternative approach**

Standard weighted average price of materials = $\dfrac{\$48}{15 \text{ litres}}$ = $3.20 per litre

| Material | Actual input<br>Litres | Standard mix<br>of actual<br>input<br>Litres | Difference<br>Litres | × difference between<br>weighted average price and<br>standard price<br>$ | Mix variance<br>$ |
|---|---|---|---|---|---|
| G | 24,500 | 27,000 | (2,500) less | ($3.20 – $4)  $0.80<br>more | 2,000 (F) |
| H | 20,500<br>45,000 | 18,000<br>45,000 | 2,500 more<br>– | ($3.20 – $2)  $1.20 | 3,000 (F)<br>5,000 (F) |

13.4 The correct answer is: 9,600 A.

| | |
|---|---|
| Total input of 45,000 litres should have yielded (÷ 15 litres) | 3,000 units |
| but did yield | 2,800 units |
| Yield variance in units | 200 units (A) |
| × standard material cost per unit of output | × $48 |
| | $9,600 A |

13.5 The correct answer is: $3,468 Adverse.

| | |
|---|---|
| (1,098 + 1,350) litres should have yielded (÷12) | 204 units |
| but did yield | 200 units |
| Yield variance in units | 4 (A) units |
| × standard cost per unit ($552 + 315) | × $867 |
| | $3,468 (A) |

13.6 The correct answer is: $120 (A)

Standard mix is $\frac{3}{8}$ grade 1, $\frac{5}{8}$ grade 2.

| Labour grade | Actual input<br>hours | Standard<br>mix of<br>actual input<br>hours | Variance<br>hours | | × standard<br>rate<br>$ | Variance<br>$ | |
|---|---|---|---|---|---|---|---|
| 1 | 2,550 | 2,490 | 60 | (A) | 8 | 480 | (A) |
| 2 | 4,090<br>6,640 | 4,150<br>6,640 | 60<br>– | (F) | 6 | 360<br>120 | (F)<br>(A) |

**Alternative approach**

| Labour<br>grade | Actual<br>input<br>hours | Standard mix<br>of actual<br>input<br>hours | Difference<br>hours | × difference between weighted<br>average rate and standard rate<br>$ | Mix<br>variance<br>$ |
|---|---|---|---|---|---|
| 1 | 2,550 | 2,490 | 60 | ($6.75* – $8)  (1.25) | 75 (A) |
| 2 | 4,090<br>6,640 | 4,150<br>6,640 | (60) | ($6.75 – $6)  0.75 | 45 (A)<br>120 (A) |

*$54/8

13.7 The correct answer is: $1,620 (A)

| | | |
|---|---|---|
| 6,640 hours of labour should yield (÷ 8 hours) | 830 | Units |
| but did yield | 800 | Units |
| Yield variance in units | 30 | Units (A) |
| × standard labour cost per unit of output | × $54 | |
| Yield variance in $ | $1,620 | (A) |

If you selected $202.50 (A) you calculated the correct yield variance in units but you evaluated it at the average standard rate per labour hour ($6.75).

If you selected $1,620 (F) you calculated the variance correctly but misinterpreted it as favourable.

$1,740 (A) is the efficiency variance, which is the total of the variances for labour mix and yield.

13.8 The correct answer is: Circumstances 2 and 3 only.

Excessive usage of materials is reported as a usage variance, not a price variance. The operational manager should be responsible for price variances when they have responsibility for materials purchasing, or when the production department asks for an urgent materials order, resulting in higher purchasing prices than normal.

13.9 The correct answer is: Material usage operational variance

Material usage variances are in the production manager's control. Material price variances are usually the responsibility of the purchasing manager.

Operational variances can be controlled by a line manager. In this instance the production manager can control efficiencies within the production process, influencing the operational variance. Planning variances are attributable to the manager responsible for approving the original standard, usually a more senior director.

13.10 The correct answer is: Sales mix variance.

The loss of the advertising campaign means that sales of Product Y will be less than budgeted, which should lead us to expect adverse sales volume variance for Y and an adverse sales quantity variance for both products together. The price discounting for Product Y should lead us to expect an adverse sales price variance. The increase in the proportion of Product X units sold in the total sales mix should lead us to expect a favourable sales mix variance, because Product X has a bigger standard contribution, both per unit and per $1 of standard sales price, than Product Y.

13.11 The correct answer is:

| Ingredient A | 44,000 kgs at standard price |
|---|---|
| Ingredient B | 31,000 kgs at standard price |
| Ingredient C | 20,000 kgs at standard price |

| Ingredient A | 47,500 kgs at standard price |
|---|---|
| Ingredient B | 28,500 kgs at standard price |
| Ingredient C | 19,000 kgs at standard price |

The mix variance should always be based on standard price. It should compare the actual quantities in the actual mix to the actual quantities in the standard mix.

# 14 Risk and uncertainty in decision making

14.1 The correct answer is: 1,000 burgers.

Maximin = maximise the minimum achievable profit. The minimum achievable profits are when the weather is bad. The maximum profit when the weather is bad is achieved when 1,000 burgers are purchased.

14.2 The correct answer is: 3,000 burgers.

Table of regrets

| | *Number of burgers purchased* | | | |
|---|---|---|---|---|
| | 1,000 | 2,000 | 3,000 | 4,000 |
| Weather | | | | |
| Bad | 0 | 1,000 | 2,000 | 4,000 |
| Average | 4,000 | 1,000 | 0 | 1,000 |
| Good | 9,000 | 6,000 | 3,000 | 0 |
| **Maximum regret** | **9,000** | **6,000** | **3,000** | **4,000** |

The lowest of these four maximum regrets is 3,000 when 3,000 burgers are purchased.

BPP LEARNING MEDIA

14.3 The correct answer is: $12 million.

At point D the alternative outcomes are to continue or abandon.

The option to continue has an expected value of:

$(0.6 \times 40) + (0.4 \times 20) = \$32m$

Less costs (20m)

EV of option $12m

14.4 The correct answer is:

Assume that the worst outcome will always occur and will select the largest payoff under this assumption.

Assuming that they will regret not having chosen another alternative and will therefore minimise the possible loss under this assumption is a minimax regret strategy.

Assuming that the best payoff will always occur and selecting the option with the largest payoff is a maximax strategy.

14.5 The correct answer is: $220,500

The expected value for fixed costs is:

$0.40 \times 100,000 + 0.35 \times 120,000 + 0.25 \times \$150,000 = \$119,500$

The expected value for variable costs is:

$0.35 \times 80,000 + 0.45 \times 100,000 + 0.20 \times \$140,000 = \$101,000$

The total expected value of costs is $119,500 + $101,000 = $220,500.

14.6 The correct answer is: $200

The regret matrix has already been drawn so it's just a case of reading off the maximum regrets for each selling price and picking the lowest one:

| Selling price | $140 | $160 | $180 | $200 |
|---|---|---|---|---|
| Maximum regret | $50,000 | $60,000 | $40,000 | $30,000 |

The lowest maximum regret is $30,000 at a selling price of $200.

14.7 The correct answer is: 2 only is correct.

Decision trees are used primarily to show decision options and decision outcomes in order to identify the decision option with the most favourable expected value. They cannot easily be used to show minimax regret values.

Decision trees may omit some possible decision options, or may simplify the possible outcomes. For example, a decision tree may show possible outcomes as 'sales demand 10,000' and 'sales demand 3,000' whereas a variety of outcomes between these two figures for sales demand may be possible. The decision tree is therefore likely to be a simplification of reality.

14.8 The correct answer is: $28,100

If the product development phase is successful the expected value is:

$0.5 \times 150,000 + 0.4 \times 50,000 + 0.1 \times (\$120,000) = \$83,000$

Note that this takes into account the cost of product development.

There is a 70% chance of this.

If the development phase fails then there will be a loss of $100,000.

There is a 30% chance of this.

So the overall expected value is:

$0.7 \times 83,000 + 0.3 \times -100,000 = 28,100$

14.9   The correct answer is: $32 (in '000s).

The best outcome without perfect information is project A with an expected value of $490 (000).

The best out come with perfect information is

- Weak demand – project C, net cash flow of $450 (000)
- Average demand – project A, net cash flow of $500 (000)
- Good demand – project B, net cash flow of $640 (000)

The expected value of these outcomes is:

- Weak demand – project C, $450 × 0.4 = 180
- Average demand – project A, $500 × 0.3 = 150
- Good demand – project B, 640 × 0.3 = 192

This adds up to 180 + 150 + 192 = $522 (000)

This is higher than the best outcome without perfect information by $32 (000). This is calculated as $522 – $490 = $32.

14.10  The correct answer:

Ignore risk when making decisions between projects that deliver the same expected value.

A 'risk neutral' decision maker will be interested in risk to the extent that it affects the expected value calculation eg if there is a high risk of a poor outcome they would take this into account in decision making. So they do not ignore risk entirely. However, if faced with two decisions with the same expected value they will not take risk of high or low returns into account when making a decision. They would be neutral between the two decisions.

'Risk-averters' try to avoid risk, and 'risk - seekers' seek risk.

14.11  The correct answer is: 8.08%

$\mu = 50cm$

$\sigma = 5cm$

$z = \dfrac{57 - 50}{5}$

= 1.4 standard deviations above the mean. Using the normal distribution tables, the proportion between the mean and 1.4 standard deviations above the mean = 0.4192

Therefore the percentage of tubes at least 57 cm long is 0.50 – 0.4192 = 0.0808 = 8.08%

14.12  The correct answer is: 21.19%

$\mu = 80kg$

$\sigma = 5kg$

$z = \dfrac{84 - 80}{5}$

= 0.8 standard deviations above the mean. Using the normal distribution tables, the proportion between the mean and 0.8 standard deviations above the mean = 0.2881

Therefore the percentage of items weighting at least 84kg is 0.50 – 0.2881 = 0.2119 = 21.19%

14.13  The correct answer is: Project C

Projects A and C both have the lowest level of risk, meaning that they would be attractive to a risk averse investor. However, project C gives a higher level of return for the same amount of risk, meaning that it would be preferable.

BPP
LEARNING MEDIA

14.14 The correct answer is: 100

| Market conditions | Probability | Purchase 100 | Purchase 200 | Purchase 300 | Purchase 400 |
|---|---|---|---|---|---|
| Weak | 15% | 50 | (100) | (200) | (250) |
| Average | 25% | 120 | 120 | 250 | 100 |
| Strong | 50% | 90 | 200 | 300 | 400 |
| Exceptional | 10% | 80 | 300 | 400 | 500 |
| Minimum return | | 50 | (100) | (200) | (250) |

Therefore choose to purchase 100 as this has the best, minimum return

14.15 The correct answer is: 400

| Market conditions | Probability | Purchase 100 | Purchase 200 | Purchase 300 | Purchase 400 |
|---|---|---|---|---|---|
| Weak | 15% | 50 | (100) | (200) | (250) |
| Average | 25% | 120 | 120 | 250 | 100 |
| Strong | 50% | 90 | 200 | 300 | 400 |
| Exceptional | 10% | 80 | 300 | 400 | 500 |
| Maximum return | | 120 | 300 | 400 | 500 |

Therefore choose to purchase 400 as this has the highest possible return.

14.16 The correct answer is: 15

| Demand | Make 5 | Make 10 | Make 15 | Make 20 |
|---|---|---|---|---|
| Poor | - | 30 | 25 | 40 |
| Average | 20 | 10 | 5 | - |
| Strong | 30 | 10 | 5 | - |
| Max regret | 30 | 30 | 25 | 40 |

Therefore choose to make 15 as this where the level of regret is lowest.

14.17 The correct answer is: $142,500

| Selling price $ | Variable cost per unit $ | Contribution per unit $ | Total contribution $ | Probability | EV $ |
|---|---|---|---|---|---|
| 70 | 60 | 10 | 100,000 | 0.35 | 35,000 |
| 70 | 55 | 15 | 150,000 | 0.45 | 67,500 |
| 70 | 50 | 20 | 200,000 | 0.20 | 40,000 |
| Total contribution | | | | | 142,500 |

Note: Fixed costs have been ignored as these are not relevant when calculating contribution.

14.18 The correct answer is: $3.2m

EV @ A: $(0.7 \times 8) + (0.3 \times -3) = 4.7m$

Less costs of developing (1.5m) = $3.2m, as this is higher than the $2m for selling, the best option is to develop product G.

14.19 The correct answer is: $6m

|  |  | $m |
|---|---|---|
| EV with perfect information | $(0.3 \times 40) + (0.5 \times 30) + (0.2 \times 30)$ | 33 |
| EV without perfect information |  | 27 |
| Value of perfect information |  | 6 |

Need to work out the highest possible EV without perfect information:

Investment 1 = $20m

Investment 2 = $(0.3 \times 40) + (0.5 \times 30)$ = $27m

Investment 3 = $(0.3 \times 5) + (0.5 \times 25) + (0.2 \times 30)$ = $20m

14.20 The correct answer is: 175

|  |  | Daily supply of sandwiches (units) | | | |
|---|---|---|---|---|---|
|  |  | 125 | 150 | 175 | 200 |
| Daily demand | 125 | $0 | $11 | $41 | $60 |
| for sandwiches | 150 | $18 | $0 | $22 | $39 |
| (units) | 175 | $41 | $20 | $0 | $17 |
|  | 200 | $71 | $45 | $26 | $0 |
| Max regret |  | 71 | 45 | 41 | 60 |

Therefore choose to supply 175 sandwiches per day as the maximum regret is lowest.

# 15 Mixed Bank 1

15.1 The correct answer is: 2 only.

Standard costing systems are not compatible with a Total Quality Management approach to operations. With standard costing, the aim is to achieve standard cost or perhaps obtain some favourable variances. With TQM, guiding principles are 'continuous improvement' and 'zero defects'. Existing standards and methods of operating are always unsatisfactory and improvements should always be sought. This is not compatible with a standard costing 'philosophy'.

Standard costing is of no value in a rapidly-changing environment because products are not standardised for a sufficient length of time to make the preparation of standard costs worthwhile.

15.2 The correct answer is:$258,948

Standard marginal costing reconciliation

|  | $ |
|---|---|
| Original budgeted contribution | 290,000 |
| Sales volume variance | (36,250) |
| Standard contribution from actual sales | 253,750 |
| Selling price variance | 21,875 |
|  | 275,625 |
| Variable cost variances |  |
| Total direct material variance | (6,335) |
| Total direct labour variance | 11,323 |
| Total variable overhead variance | (21,665) |
| Actual contribution | 258,948 |

BPP LEARNING MEDIA

15.3 The correct answer is: Product X.

| | W | X | Y | Z |
|---|---|---|---|---|
| | $ | $ | $ | $ |
| | per unit | per unit | per unit | per unit |
| Selling price | 56 | 67 | 89 | 96 |
| Material | 22 | 31 | 38 | 46 |
| Throughput contribution | 34 | 36 | 51 | 50 |
| Time on bottleneck resource | 10 | 10 | 15 | 15 |
| Product return per minute | $3.40 | $3.60 | $3.40 | $3.33 |
| Ranking | 2 | 1 | 2 | 4 |

15.4 The correct answer is: Replacement cost.

The relevant cost is the replacement cost of the material because material X is used regularly by the company in its normal business and is available from inventory.

15.5 The correct answers are:

- The sales value of the joint product at the separation point
- The final sales value of the joint product
- The further processing cost of the joint product

Incorrect answers:

- The value of the common process costs
- The method of apportioning the common costs between the joint products

These are not relevant because the common costs remain unaltered regardless of whether the joint products are processed further.

15.6 The correct answer is: $450,000

Contribution per mix = ($30 × 4) + ($25 × 3) = $195

Breakeven point in terms of mixes = Fixed cost / contribution per mix

= $975,000 / $195
= 5, 000 mixes

Breakeven point in units

A     5,000 × 4 = 20,000 units
B     5,000 × 3 = 15,000 units

Breakeven point in revenue

A     20,000 × $40 = $800,000
B     15,000 × $50 = $750,000

Total = $800,000 + $750,000 = $1,550,000

Margin of safety = budgeted sales − breakeven sales

= $2,000,000 − $1,550,000
= $450,000

15.7 The correct answer is: 675 units.

Forecast sales before seasonal adjustment = (53 × 17) − 258 = 643

Forecast sales after seasonal adjustment = 643 × 105% = 675 units

15.8 The correct answer is: $1,470 (A)

Standard hours per unit = 600/400 = 1.5

| Original standard cost = 490 units × 1.5 × $25 | $18,375 |
|---|---|
| Revised standard cost = 490 units × 1.5 × $27 | $19,845 |
| Labour rate planning variance | $1,470 (A) |

**15.9** The correct answer is: Neither 1 nor 2.

Mix and yield variances measure costs and output quantities, not quality. A potential problem is that persistent favourable mix variances may have an adverse effect on sales volume variances and direct labour efficiency variances, because the cheaper materials mix may affect the quality of the product sold to customers and also make the product more difficult to handle. These consequences could lead to adverse sales volume and labour efficiency variances.

**15.10** The correct answer is: 104,000 units.

If the probability of a dry summer is 0.4 and the probability of a wet summer is 0.6. Therefore the expected value for sales is calculated as $0.6 \times 120,000 + 0.4 \times 80,000 = 104,000$.

# 16 Mixed Bank 2

**16.1** The correct answer is: 2 only.

Standard costing is not well suited to production where items are made to customer specifications. This is because items are not produced to standard specifications on which a standard cost can be based.

Similarly, standard costing is not consistent with a philosophy of continuous improvement and TQM, because if improvements are continually achieved, the standard costs will have to be continually reviewed and revised.

**16.2** The correct answer is: Both statements are true.

Remember that the over or under absorbed overhead is made up of the fixed overhead expenditure variance, the fixed overhead efficiency variance and the fixed overhead capacity variance.

**16.3** The correct answer is: $75,000 lower.

Inventory reduction of 300 units

Budgeted overhead absorption $\dfrac{\$500,000}{2,000}$ = $250 per unit

Reduction in profit:

300 units × $250 per unit = $75,000

**16.4** The correct answer is: $25,230.

420 of the units required are already in stock. There are two alternative uses for these units.

They can be sold to realise $420 \times \$30 = \$12,600$, or they can be used as a substitute for material V. The saving would be $750 \times \$25 = \$18,750$.

This is therefore the best alternative use for the stock of material S. The opportunity cost of using them is the saving foregone. The remaining units will have to be purchased.

The relevant cost is $\$18,750 + (90 \times \$72) = \$25,230$.

**16.5** The correct answers are:

- The costs of further processing
- The quantity of losses expected from further processing and their sales value
- The sales value prior to further processing
- The sales value after further processing

When deciding whether or not to further process a joint product after the separation point we do not require information on the joint process. The information we require relates to further processing.

**16.6** The correct answer is: $2J + 1.5T \leq 2,325$.

Let Jackets = J and Trousers = T.

The total available is 2,800m. However, 475m is required for the contract $(200 \times 2 + 50 \times 1.5)$ and therefore the amount to be considered in the decision is reduced to 2,325. The correct answer is therefore $2J + 1.5T \leq 2,325$.

BPP
LEARNING MEDIA

If you chose 2J + 1.5T ≤ 2,800 you did not deduct the amount required for the special contract. If you chose 2J + 1.5T ≤ 3,275 you added the amount required for the special contract on to the total requirement incorrectly instead of deducting it.

If you chose 1.5J+ 2T ≤ 2,325 you mixed up T and J in your resource requirements.

16.7 The correct answer is: 300,750 units

The forecast for sales units for the third quarter of year 7 is 300,750

Assuming that the first quarter of year one is time period reference number 1, the third quarter of year 7 is time reference X = (6 years × 4 quarters) + 3 quarters = 27

Therefore the trend Y =  25,000 + (6,500 × 27) = 200,500

Seasonally adjusted for the sales value of quarter 3

Y  = 200,500 × 150% = 300,750 units

16.8 The correct answer is: $3,240 (F).

Total actual sales = 5,800 + 2,700 + 1,800 = $10,300

Actual sales in standard mix:

| | | |
|---|---|---|
| X | $10,300 × 5/10 = | $5,150 |
| Y | $10,300 × 3/10 = | $3,090 |
| Z | $10,300 × 2/10 = | $2,060 |
| | | $10,300 |

| | Actual sales Std mix $ | Std sales Std mix $ | Diff in units | × std profit $ | Variance $ |
|---|---|---|---|---|---|
| X | 5,150 | 5,000 | 150 (F) | 8 | 1,200 (F) |
| Y | 3,090 | 3,000 | 90 (F) | 14 | 1,260 (F) |
| Z | 2,060 | 2,000 | 60 (F) | 16 | 960 (F) |
| | | | | | 3,420 (F) |

16.9 The correct answer is: $1,475 (A).

Sales mix variance

| | Actual sales Std mix (W1) | Actual qty Act mix | Difference in units | | × std profit $ | Variance $ | |
|---|---|---|---|---|---|---|---|
| X | 750 | 700 | 50 | (A) | 10 | 500 | (A) |
| Y | 937.5 | 1,200 | 262.5 | (F) | 6 | 1,575 | (F) |
| Z | 562.5 | 350 | 212.5 | (A) | 12 | 2,550 | (A) |
| | 2,250 | 2,250 | – | | | 1,475 | (A) |

Working

Actual sales at std mix:

| | | |
|---|---|---|
| X | 2,250 × (800/2,400) = | 750 |
| Y | 2,250 × (1,000/2,400) = | 937.5 |
| Z | 2,250 × (600/2,400) = | 562.5 |

16.10 The correct answer is: 0.51

A profit of $1,000 and a loss of $3,000 are less than or equal to a profit of $1,000 and so the overall probability of a profit of $1,000 or less is 0.3 + 0.21 = 0.51.

# 17 Mixed Bank 3

17.1 The correct answer is: 1 is true and 2 is false.

Statement 1 is true. Statement 2 is false. Producing 5,000 standard hours of work in 5,500 hours would give rise to an adverse fixed overhead volume efficiency variance.

17.2 The correct answer is: $286.76.

| | $ per unit |
|---|---|
| Material | 20.00 |
| Labour | 69.40 |
| Production overhead (14 hours × $12.58) | 176.12 |
| Total production cost | 265.52 |
| General overhead (8% of $265.52) | 21.24 |
| Total cost | 286.76 |

17.3 The correct answer is: $3,100.

First calculate the number of units of inventory left at the end of October.

Closing inventory units = Opening inventory units + units produced − units sold.

= 0 + 4,000 − 3,600

= 400

The value of inventory using marginal costing is:

| | $ |
|---|---|
| Direct material | 20,000 |
| Direct labour | 6,300 |
| Variable production overhead | 4,700 |
| | 31,000 |

Cost per unit = $31,000/4,000 = $7.75

400 units cost 400 × $7.75 = $3,100

17.4 The correct answer is: Both 1 and 2.

These are fundamental statements about relevant costing.

17.5 The correct answer is: $53,410.

| | $ | $ |
|---|---|---|
| Sales (480,000 × 1.15 × 0.97) | | 535,440 |
| Direct materials (140,000 × 1.15 × 0.98) | 157,780 | |
| Direct labour 110,000 + (110,000 × 0.15 × 1.50) | 134,750 | |
| Variable overheads (50,000 × 1.15) | 57,500 | |
| Fixed overheads | 132,000 | |
| Total costs | | 482,030 |
| Profit | | 53,410 |

17.6 The correct answer is: $209,500

$210,000 + $3,000 − $5,000 + $9,000 − $7,500 = $209,500.

| | | |
|---|---|---|
| Budgeted profit | not required | |
| Sales volume variance | not needed | |
| Standard profit on actual sales | 209,500 | |
| Sales price variance | 7,500 | favourable |
| Total variable cost variance | 9,000 | adverse |
| Fixed cost expenditure variance | 5,000 | favourable |
| Fixed cost volume variance | 3,000 | adverse |
| Actual profit | 210,000 | |

BPP
LEARNING MEDIA

**17.7** The correct answer is: $21,826

| | | |
|---|---|---|
| High activity | 2,400 | 23,170 |
| Low activity | 1,650 | 20,770 |
| | 750 | 2,400 |

Variable cost per unit = $\dfrac{\$2,400}{750}$ = $3.20 per unit

Fixed cost (substituting in high activity)    = $23,170 – (2,400 × $3.20)
                                           = $15,490

Budget cost allowance for 1,980 units

| | $ |
|---|---|
| Variable cost (1,980 × $3.20) | 6,336 |
| Fixed cost | 15,490 |
| | 21,826 |

Remember that you are dealing with **fixed** costs as well as variable costs. Do not make the mistake of dividing the total cost for production of 1,650 units by 1,650 to get a 'cost per unit' and then multiplying this cost by 1,980 to get the cost of 1,980 units. This would be a valid approach if you are dealing with variable costs only.

Similarly do not divide the total cost for production of 2,400 units by 2,400 to get a 'cost per unit' and then multiply this cost by 1,980 to get the cost of 1,980 units. Again this would be a valid approach if you are dealing with variable costs only.

You are dealing with a mix of **both** types of cost and you therefore first have to isolate the **variable** costs from the fixed costs.

**17.8** The correct answer is: $17,600

| | | | Difference |
|---|---|---|---|
| Output | 2,000 units | 3,500 units | 1,500 units |
| Total cost | $12,000 | $16,200 | $4,200 |

Variable cost per unit = $\dfrac{\$4,200}{1,500}$ = $2.80

Fixed cost = $12,000 – (2,000 × $2.80) = $6,400

The budgeted cost allowance for 4,000 units = $6,400 + (4,000 × $2.80) = $17,600

**17.9** The correct answer is: Both 1 and 2.

If the sales mix is not a controllable item, and managers do not have control over it, sales mix variances do not provide meaningful control information. Sales volume variances for individual products would be more appropriate. If a company is trying to encourage customers to shift from one product to another, sales mix variances could provide useful control information, although other measures of performance might be just as good and possibly more suitable.

**17.10** The correct answer is: 0.82

| Demand (a) Units | Probability (b) | Revenue (a)×$45 $'000 | Variable cost per unit (c) $ | Probability (d) | Total variable costs (a)×(c) $'000 | Contribution $'000 | Joint probability (b)×(d) |
|---|---|---|---|---|---|---|---|
| 100,000 | 0.45 | 4,500 | 20 | 0.40 | 2,000 | 2,500 | 0.18 |
| 100,000 | 0.45 | 4,500 | 18 | 0.60 | 1,800 | 2,700* | 0.27 |
| 120,000 | 0.55 | 5,400 | 20 | 0.40 | 2,400 | 3,000* | 0.22 |
| 120,000 | 0.55 | 5,400 | 18 | 0.60 | 2,160 | 3,240* | 0.33 |
| | | | | | | | 1.00 |

\* Contribution higher than current level of contribution of $90,000 × $(50 – 21) = $2,610,000

∴ Probability = 0.27 + 0.22 + 0.33 = 0.82

# 18 Mixed Bank 4

18.1   The correct answers are:

- Achieving maximum capacity utilisation.

- Relying on a wide range of suppliers for raw materials and components, to ensure immediate availability of items.

JIT operations use pull scheduling, Kanban control and greater visibility in the work place. Pull scheduling (only producing for the next stage in the chain when the work is needed) results in a sacrifice of capacity utilisation. Supporters of JIT argue that it is better to be idle than to work on producing items for inventory. JIT purchasing systems rely on selecting a small number of reliable suppliers for key items, and involving these suppliers in the JIT planning and purchase ordering system.

18.2   The correct answer is: $0.40

Machining costs = $(3 \times 100,000) / [(3 \times 100,000) + (2 \times 150,000)] \times \$30,000 = \$15,000$

Set up = $(100,000 / 500) / [(100,000 / 500) + (150,000 / 500)] \times \$40,000 = \$16,000$

General admin = 100k / 250k × $10,000 = $4,000

Checking = 200 / 800 × $20,000 = $5,000

Total overhead for M = $40,000

Overhead per unit = $40,000 / 100,000 units = $0.40 per unit

18.3   The correct answer is: Lower.

Marginal costing will report a lower profit.

18.4   The correct answer is: There are two breakeven points: $5.64 million and $6.36 million.

|  | $ |
|---|---|
| Total cost at sales of $6.8 million | 6,560,000 |
| Deduct step increase in fixed costs | (400,000) |
| Total cost excluding step cost increase | 6,160,000 |
| Total cost at sales of $5.2 million | 5,440,000 |
| Therefore variable cost of sales of $1.6 million | 720,000 |

Variable cost = 720,000/1,600,000 = 45% of sales. Contribution/sales ratio is 55%.

|  | $ |
|---|---|
| Total cost at sales of $6.8 million | 6,560,000 |
| Variable cost (45%) | (3,060,000) |
| Fixed cost | 3,500,000 |

Fixed costs are $3.5 million at the higher sales level and so $3.1 million at the lower sales level.

When fixed costs are $3.1 million, breakeven sales = $3.1 million/0.55 = $5.636 million.

When fixed costs are $3.5 million, breakeven sales = $3.5 million/0.55 = $6.363 million.

18.5   The correct answer is: $300.

Contribution per hour is after deducting labour and variable overhead costs, so these are relevant costs.

|  | $ |
|---|---|
| Cost of labour (10 hours × $12) | 120 |
| Cost of variable overhead (at $3) | 30 |
| Contribution forgone (at $15) | 150 |
| Relevant cost total | 300 |

BPP
LEARNING MEDIA

18.6 The correct answer is:

Slack occurs when the **maximum** availability of a resource is not used in the optimal solution. Surplus occurs when there is production excess of a **minimum** requirement. If there is no slack then the constraints are said to be **binding**.

18.7 The correct answer is: 315.63

| Quarter | Sales | 4 Quarter Moving Average | Centred Moving Average (Trend) |
|---------|-------|--------------------------|--------------------------------|
| 1 | 300 | | |
| 2 | 320 | | |
| | | 293.75 | |
| 3 | 275 | | 298.75 |
| | | 303.75 | |
| 4 | 280 | | 308.125 |
| | | 312.50 | |
| 5 | 340 | | 315.63 |
| | | 318.75 | |
| 6 | 355 | | |
| 7 | 300 | | |

Therefore the trend figure for 1st quarter year 2 = 315.63

18.8 The correct answer is:

- a budget which, by recognising different cost behaviour patterns, is designed to change as volume of activity changes.

Flexible budgets are designed to flex with the level of activity.

A budget for a 12 month period is a fixed budget and used for planning. A rolling budget is updated but not in response to the level of activity, rather changes in the environment.

A flexible budget includes all cost types. Semi-variable costs have to be broken down but the flexed budget allowance will include total cost at that level of activity.

18.9 The correct answer is:

Planning variances represent the difference between an **original standard**, which is no longer considered to be a **relevant** or accurate target, and a **revised** standard. Planning variances therefore represent differences between target and actual performance which are **not controllable** by operational management and so there is little to be gained from focusing management control action on such variances. An operating variance, on the other hand, represents the difference between a **revised**, realistic target and actual performance and as such are deemed **controllable** by operational management. They therefore provide useful information for management control action.

18.10 The correct answer is: 63%

The probability of monthly contribution > $13,500 = 0.08 + 0.2 + 0.07 + 0.175 + 0.105 = 0.63.

| Selling price | Probability | Cost per unit | Probability | Combined probability | Monthly contribution* |
|---|---|---|---|---|---|
| $/unit | | $ | | | $ |
| 20 | 0.25 | 8 | 0.20 | 0.050 | 12,000 |
| | 0.25 | 10 | 0.50 | 0.125 | 10,000 |
| | 0.25 | 12 | 0.30 | 0.075 | 8,000 |
| 25 | 0.40 | 8 | 0.20 | 0.080 | 17,000 |
| | 0.40 | 10 | 0.50 | 0.200 | 15,000 |
| | 0.40 | 12 | 0.30 | 0.120 | 13,000 |
| 30 | 0.35 | 8 | 0.20 | 0.070 | 22,000 |
| | 0.35 | 10 | 0.50 | 0.175 | 20,000 |
| | 0.35 | 12 | 0.30 | 0.105 | 18,000 |
| | | | | 1.000 | |

* (selling price – variable cost) × 1,000

# 19 Mixed Bank 5

19.1 The correct answers are:

- Distinguishing the business from its competitors
- Driving down energy costs
- Improving corporate reputation
- Attracting new customers who are looking for zero carbon footprint alternatives
- Improving employee morale and employee performance

The two incorrect answers will increase the use of greenhouse gases.

This probably seems like an easy question when written in this format where you just have to tick the boxes. In the ICS exam, however, you may be asked to think of reasons why a business would benefit from reducing its greenhouse gases. You need to be able to think of these types of reasons for yourself and relate them to the particular business which is given in the question. You could use the mnemonic CREAM. Competition, Reputation, Energy savings (cost), Alternatives, Morale

19.2 The correct answer is: $0.90

| | | |
|---|---|---|
| Cost per movement | = $75,000/30,000 | = $2.50 |
| Number of movements per batch | | = 18 |
| Cost of movements per batch | = $2.50 × 18 | = $45 |
| Cost of movements per chair | = $45/50 | = $0.90 |

19.3 The correct answer is: 3.41

Throughput contribution per unit of J = $40 - $10 = $30

Throughput contribution per bottleneck hour = $30/0.01 hours = $3,000

Factory costs per year (overheads + labour costs) = $2,920,000 + (50,000 x $12) = $3,520,000

Factory cost per bottleneck hour = $3,520,000/4,000 hours = $880

Throughput accounting ratio = $3,000/$880 = 3.41

BPP LEARNING MEDIA

**19.4** The correct answer is: $914

| Product | A | B | C | Total |
|---|---|---|---|---|
| | $'000 | $'000 | $'000 | $'000 |
| Sales revenue | 360 | 720 | 200 | 1,280 |
| Variable costs | 90 | 240 | 110 | 440 |
| Contribution | 270 | 480 | 90 | 840 |
| Fixed costs | 180 | 360 | 60 | 600 |

Contribution/sales ratio $\quad = 840/1,280 \quad = 0.65625$

Breakeven point in sales revenue $\quad = \$600,000/0.65625 \quad = \$914,286$

With CVP analysis for a company that sells several products, a fixed sales mix has to be assumed.

**19.5** The correct answers are:

| | S | A | T |
|---|---|---|---|
| Make | 4,000 | 0 | 3,000 |
| Buy | 0 | 4,000 | 1,000 |

| | S | A | T |
|---|---|---|---|
| VC to make $ | 20 | 36 | 24 |
| Cost to buy $ | 29 | 40 | 34 |
| Incremental cost to buy $ | 9 | 4 | 10 |
| Hours to make | 3 | 2 | 4 |
| Additional cost to buy per hour | 3 | 2 | 2.5 |
| Rank to make | 1 | 3 | 2 |

Only 24,000 hours are available, therefore need to make best use of these.

| | | |
|---|---|---|
| Hours available | | 24,000 |
| 1 | Make 4,000 S @ 3 hours | (12,000) |
| 2 | Make 3,000 T @ 4 hours | (12,000) |
| | | 0 |

The remaining 1,000 units of T and 4,000 units of A will have to be bought.

The organisation's budget calls for 36,000 hours of machine time, if all the components are to be produced in-house. Only 24,000 hours are available, and so there is a shortfall of 12,000 hours of machine time, which is therefore a limiting factor. The shortage can be overcome by subcontracting the equivalent of 12,000 machine hours' output to the subcontractor.

The assembly costs are not relevant costs because they are not affected by the decision. The decision rule is to minimise the extra variable costs of subcontracting per unit of scarce resource saved (that is, per machine hour saved).

**19.6** The correct answer is: $5,060 lower

If marginal costing is used to value inventory instead of absorption costing, the difference in profits will be equal to the change in inventory volume multiplied by the fixed production overhead absorption rate = 110 units × $46 = $5,060

Since closing inventory are higher than opening inventories, the marginal costing profit will be lower that the absorption costing profit (so $5,060 higher is incorrect). This is because the marginal costing profit does not 'benefit' from the increase in the amount of fixed production overhead taken to inventory (rather than to the statement of profit or loss).

If you selected $4,600 lower or higher, you based the difference on 100 units of opening inventory.

19.7 The correct answer is:   Materials required for production – opening inventory of materials + closing inventory of materials

It may help you to think in terms of the inputs to a material purchases budget (opening inventory and purchases) and the outputs (closing inventory and the quantity used in production). The inputs should equal the outputs. Any one of the inputs or outputs can then be determined by manipulating opening inventory + purchases = closing inventory + used in production.

19.8 The correct answer is: $24,450 A.

|  | $ |
|---|---|
| 2,445 units (actual sales) should sell for @ $400 | 978,000 |
| 2,445 units did sell for @ $390 | 953,550 |
| Variance | 24,450 A |

19.9 The correct answer is: Statement 2 only.

Mix variances can only be calculated when a product contains two or more materials that can be mixed together in different proportions. For example, calculating a mix variance for the production of a bicycle out of its component parts would be meaningless. It is important to be aware of the interdependence between variances: a favourable mix variance, meaning a cheaper mix of materials in a product, may result in adverse total output of the product (adverse yield).

However, it is not the case that a favourable mix variance will always result in an adverse yield variance.

19.10 The correct answer is: $2,100,000

Contribution = Selling price – variable cost

= $120 – $40

= $80

Total contribution = 40,000 members × $80 = $3,200,000

Profit = $3,200,000 – $1,100,000 = $2,100,000

# 20 Mixed Bank 6

20.1 The correct answers are:

- It is not always easy to predict patterns of demand.
- JIT makes the organisation far more vulnerable to disruptions in the supply chain.
- Wide geographical spread makes JIT difficult.

There is not a danger of inventory becoming obsolete as raw materials will only be purchased when they are needed for production and production is driven by demand for finished products. The minimal inventory levels mean that there is much less chance of obsolescence. The fact that JIT is demand led system is actually a benefit rather than a problem.

20.2 The correct answers are:

- Allocate overheads to cost objects.
- Allocate overheads to primary and support activities.

Production and service cost centres are features of absorption costing not ABC.

In no costing system are overheads allocated to resources.

BPP
LEARNING MEDIA

20.3    The correct answer is: 12,500

Any difference between marginal and absorption costing profit is due to changes in inventory.

| | |
|---|---|
| Absorption costing profit | $2,000 |
| Marginal costing loss | $(3,000) |
| Difference | $5,000 |

Change in inventory = Difference in profit/fixed product cost per unit:

= $5,000/$2 = 2,500 units.

Marginal costing loss is lower than absorption costing profit therefore inventory has gone up – that is, production was greater than sales by 2,500 units.

Production = 10,000 units (sales) + 2,500 units = 12,500 units.

20.4    The correct answer is: $5.188 million.

Weighted average sales price per unit = $[(20 \times 2) + (18 \times 3) + (24 \times 5)]/(2 + 3 + 5) = \$21.40$

Weighted average variable cost per unit = $[(11 \times 2) + (12 \times 3) + (18 \times 5)]/(2 + 3 + 5) = \$14.80$

Therefore weighted average contribution per unit = $\$(21.40 - 14.80) = \$6.60$

Weighted average C/S ratio = 6.60/21.40 = 0.3084112

Sales required to achieve target contribution of $1.6 million = $1.6 million/0.3084112 = $5.188 million.

If you chose $4.724m. You did not weight the sales and variable costs and so came up with a simple average contribution of 21 (C/S ratio of 0.3387).

If you chose $5.011m then you correctly calculated the average contribution of $6.60 and the BE mixes as 242.42. You then multiplied this by the simple average of $20.67 (not the weighted average) to get to the BE revenue.

If you chose $3.891m you forgot to add the target profit figure on.

20.5    The correct answer is: $170

X is used regularly, so relevant cost = current cost = $100

Y is not currently used, disposal cost saved = $30

Z is not currently used, refund lost = $100

Overall cost = $100 - $30 + $100 = $170.

20.6    The correct answer is $5,000 Adverse

Standard fixed overhead absorption rate per hour = $125,000/25,000 = $5 per hour

Fixed overhead volume capacity variance

| | |
|---|---|
| Budgeted hours of work | 25,000 hrs |
| Actual hours of work | 24,000 hrs |
| Fixed overhead volume capacity variance | 1,000 hrs (A) |
| x standard fixed overhead absorption rate per hour | × $5 |
| Fixed overhead volume capacity variance in $ | $5,000 (A) |

20.7    The correct answer is: The budgeted statement of cash flow, budgeted statement of profit or loss and the budgeted statement of financial position.

It does not necessarily contain all of the budgets prepared.

20.8    The correct answer is: There is a favourable variance on labour costs, and contribution is lower than should
        have been expected.

| Actual cost of labour | = | $9,200 |
|---|---|---|
| Expected cost of labour for a production level of 12,000 units | = | $8,000 × 12,000/10,000 |
|  | = | $9,600 |
| Variance | = | $400 F |
| Expected contribution for a production level of 12,000 units | = | $29,000 × 12/10 |
|  | = | $34,800 |
| Actual contribution | = | $32,900 |

        Therefore, contribution is lower than should have been expected.

20.9    The correct answer is: $49.20 Favourable.

        Product TRD100

|  | Standard mix | Actual mix | Difference | Price | Variance |  |
|---|---|---|---|---|---|---|
|  | Litres | Litres | Litres | $ | $ |  |
| X | 885.6 | 984 | 98.4 | 2.50 | 246.0 | (A) |
| Y | 1,328.4 | 1,230 | 98.4 | 3.00 | 295.2 | (F) |
| Total | 2,214.0 | 2,214 | nil |  | 49.2 | (F) |

20.10   The correct answer is: Choice 4.

        EV of Choice 1 = $9,500

        EV of Choice 2 = (0.3 × 14,000) + (0.3 × 10,000) + (0.4 × 5,000) = $9,200

        EV of Choice 3 = (0.4 × 10,000) + (0.6 × 9,000) = $9,400

        EV of Choice 4 = (0.7 × 8,000) + (0.3 × 14,000) = $9,800

# 21 Mixed Bank 7

21.1    The correct answers are:

        •   Quality and reliability
        •   Flexibility
        •   Customer satisfaction

        WCM incorporates the principles of Total Quality Management.

        WCM aims to know what customer requirements are, to supply customers reliably and on time and to change
        products/develop new products as customer needs change.

        It may be necessary to exceed the target cost and generate adverse variances to ensure that the desired level
        of quality and customer satisfaction are obtained.

21.2    The correct answer is: $2,136

|  | $ |
|---|---|
| Budgeted recovery of costs ($97,500/3,250) × 267 | 8,010 |
| Actual costs | 10,146 |
| Under recovery | 2,136 |

        If you selected $34,398: You multiplied the period 10 cost by 13 to get an 'annual' cost, and compared this
        with the budgeted total cost.

BPP
LEARNING MEDIA

**21.3** The correct answer is: X, W and Y.

Total labour hours required to meet sales budget: $(10,000 + 6,250 + 15,000 + 10,000) = 41,250$.

Direct labour hours are therefore a limiting factor on production.

| Product | W | X | Y | Z |
|---|---|---|---|---|
| Contribution per unit | $3.5 | $2.0 | $1.8 | $4.0 |
| Direct labour hours per unit | 0.5 | 0.25 | 0.3 | 0.8 |
| Contribution per direct labour hour | $7 | $8 | $6 | $5 |
| Priority for manufacture and sales | 2nd | 1st | 3rd | 4th |

So make and sell 25,000 units of X (6,250 hours), 20,000 units of W (10,000 hours) and 25,833.33 units of Y with the remaining 7,750 hours available.

**21.4** The correct answer is: $2,802

When sales revenue is $1.5 million, total contribution is $45\% \times \$1.5$ million = $675,000.

This leaves a further $625,000 of fixed costs to cover. To achieve breakeven, sales in excess of $1.5 million need to be $625,000/0.48 = $1.302 million.

Total sales to achieve breakeven = $1.5 million + $1.302 million = $2.802 million

**21.5** The correct answers are:

- Loss of control. By outsourcing part of the production process the company is effectively handing over control of issues such as quality to a third party.

- Loss of competitive advantage. An outsourcing partner can make the same parts and components for other competitors meaning that if too much of the production process is outsourced then competitive advantage can be lost.

- Loss of in-house skill. Shutting down parts of the factory and handing it over to an outsource company is likely to lead to a reduction in staff. This can make the decision to outsource hard to reverse.

Additional note: The decision to outsource can enable an organisation to tap into specialist knowledge which it does not currently possess. In addition it is likely to free up production capacity and reduce the amount of capital required.

**21.6** The correct answer is: $32.50

The shadow price for material X is the contribution that can be generated per m.

This is the unit contribution of $65 divided by the number of metres (2) = $32.50

**21.7** The correct answer is: All of the statements can be used to describe ABB.

ABB can be applied on a number of levels and hence various definitions are appropriate.

**21.8** The correct answer is: Standard profit margin.

The sales volume profit variance is calculated as the difference between budgeted sales volume and actual sales volume, valued at the standard profit margin per unit. This approach is used when the company uses absorption costing. Under marginal costing the difference in units is valued at the standard contribution margin.

**21.9** The correct answer is: $151.20 Adverse.

| | | |
|---|---|---|
| Expected output of product TRD100 $\dfrac{2,214}{30}$ | = | 73.8 units |
| Actual output | = | 72.0 units |
| Shortfall | = | 1.8 units |
| 1.8 units × $84/unit | = | $151.20(A) |

BPP
LEARNING MEDIA

**21.10** The correct answer is: $70

The worst outcome under each decision is as follows

| Selling price | $60 | $70 | $80 | $90 |
|---|---|---|---|---|
| Demand level | | | | |
| | $'000s | $'000s | $'000s | $'000s |
| Weak | 20 | 35 | 20 | 10 |

Using the maximin criterion, the best of these outcomes is 35, and this is achieved by selecting $70 as the selling price.

# 22 Mixed Bank 8

**22.1** The correct answers are:

- Administration of quality control
- Maintenance of inspection equipment
- Training in quality control

Performance testing is an appraisal cost. Costs of repair under warranty are external failure costs.

**22.2** The correct answer is: $0.15

Number of batches produced

| L | 200,000/200 | 1,000 |
|---|---|---|
| D | 200,000/100 | 2,000 |
| S | 100,000/50 | 2,000 |

Number of set-ups required

| L | 1,000 × 2 | 2,000 |
|---|---|---|
| D | 2,000 × 3 | 6,000 |
| S | 2,000 × 5 | 10,000 |
| | | = 18,000 |

Cost per set-up = $270,000/18,000 = $15

Machine set-up cost per batch of L = $15 × 2 = $30

Cost per unit of L = $30/200 = $0.15

$30: is the set-up cost per batch of L.

$15: is the cost per set-up.

$0.54: is found by dividing the total cost by the total production level of 500,000 units.

**22.3** The correct answer is: Marginal costing.

This is because it focuses on incremental costs. Total absorption and activity based costing involve notional costs (such as depreciation) and fixed costs (such as rent), which are never relevant to a decision. Standard costing does not necessarily deal with actual cash flow and is so unlikely to produce useful decision-making information.

**22.4** The correct answer is: $42,300

**Contribution per unit**

| A | $22 |
|---|---|
| B | $19 |
| C | $17 |

BPP LEARNING MEDIA

**Contribution per mix**

($22 × 1) + ($19 × 1) + ($17 × 4) = $109

**Required number of mixes**

(Fixed costs + required profit)/contribution per mix     = $(55,100 + 43,000)/$109

= 900 mixes

**Required sales of A**

900 × 1      = 900 units
900 × $47    = $42,300 revenue

22.5   The correct answer is: No product should be discontinued.

Much of the fixed overhead apportioned to each product is actually general overhead and would exist even if production ceased. The profits for each product can be recalculated as follows deducting only costs which relate to the products:

|  | K $'000 | L $'000 | G $'000 | Total $'000 |
|---|---|---|---|---|
| Sales | 600 | 400 | 300 | 1,300 |
| Cost of production |  |  |  |  |
| Materials | (200) | (100) | (85) | (385) |
| Labour | (95) | (20) | (80) | (195) |
| Variable overhead | (75) | (10) | (20) | (105) |
| Specific fixed overhead | (90) | (40) | (12) | (142) |
| Selling costs | (30) | (20) | (50) | (100) |
| Profit before general fixed overheads | 110 | 210 | 53 | 373 |
| General fixed overhead |  |  |  | (308) |
| Net profit |  |  |  | 65 |
| General overhead previously apportioned to each product |  |  |  |  |
| @ 80% of material cost | (160) | (80) | (68) | (308) |

Each product therefore generates a profit before general overheads. This means that ceasing production of any of the products would lead to a fall in profits.

22.6   The correct answer is: 0

The resource is not scarce and as such there is no shadow price.

22.7   The correct answer is: There are no performance targets for managers.

The answer is that there are no performance targets for managers. There are usually performance targets in a budget, but with incremental budgeting these are often not challenging. There is no incentive with incremental budgeting for managers to reduce costs; on the contrary, there is an incentive for managers to make sure that they spend up to their budget limit in order to retain the spending in next year's budget.

22.8   The correct answer is: $1,270 adverse.

| Total variance | = expenditure variance + volume variance |
|---|---|
| Expenditure variance | = actual expenditure – budgeted expenditure |
|  | = $(177,770 – 170,000) |
|  | = $7,770 (A) |
| Total variance | = $(7,770(A) + 6,500(F)) |
|  | = $1,270(A) |

**22.9** The correct answer is: 40 (F).

|  | Kg |
|---|---|
| 120 units of product should use (× 3.5 kg) | 420 |
| They did use | 410 |
| Operational usage variance in kg | 10 (F) |

Operational usage variance in $ (× standard price per kg $4) = $40 (F)

**22.10** The correct answer:

Maximum regret (best outcome - actual outcome) is as follows

*Payoff table*                                      *Units produced*

|  | **Best outcome** | 200 units | 210 units | 220 units |
|---|---|---|---|---|
| Demand |  |  |  |  |
| 200 units | **12,000** | 0 | 12,000 – 11,600 = 400 | 12,000 – 11,200 = 800 |
| 210 units | **12,600** | 12,600 – 12,000 = 600 | 0 | 12,600 – 12,200 = 400 |
| 220 units | **13,200** | 13,200 – 12,000 = 1,200 | 13,200 – 12,600 = 600 | 0 |

As a footnote - the best decision using the minimax regret rule is to produce 210 units which has the lowest maximum regret (600).

BPP LEARNING MEDIA

# Mathematical tables

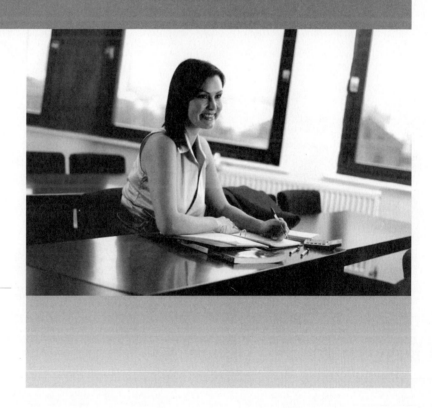

BPP
LEARNING MEDIA

BPP
LEARNING MEDIA

# PRESENT VALUE TABLE

Present value of 1.00 unit of currency, that is $(1+r)^{-n}$ where $r$ = interest rate; $n$ = number of periods until payment or receipt.

| Periods (n) | Interest rates (r) | | | | | | | | | |
|---|---|---|---|---|---|---|---|---|---|---|
| | 1% | 2% | 3% | 4% | 5% | 6% | 7% | 8% | 9% | 10% |
| 1 | 0.990 | 0.980 | 0.971 | 0.962 | 0.952 | 0.943 | 0.935 | 0.926 | 0.917 | 0.909 |
| 2 | 0.980 | 0.961 | 0.943 | 0.925 | 0.907 | 0.890 | 0.873 | 0.857 | 0.842 | 0.826 |
| 3 | 0.971 | 0.942 | 0.915 | 0.889 | 0.864 | 0.840 | 0.816 | 0.794 | 0.772 | 0.751 |
| 4 | 0.961 | 0.924 | 0.888 | 0.855 | 0.823 | 0.792 | 0.763 | 0.735 | 0.708 | 0.683 |
| 5 | 0.951 | 0.906 | 0.863 | 0.822 | 0.784 | 0.747 | 0.713 | 0.681 | 0.650 | 0.621 |
| 6 | 0.942 | 0.888 | 0.837 | 0.790 | 0.746 | 0.705 | 0.666 | 0.630 | 0.596 | 0.564 |
| 7 | 0.933 | 0.871 | 0.813 | 0.760 | 0.711 | 0.665 | 0.623 | 0.583 | 0.547 | 0.513 |
| 8 | 0.923 | 0.853 | 0.789 | 0.731 | 0.677 | 0.627 | 0.582 | 0.540 | 0.502 | 0.467 |
| 9 | 0.914 | 0.837 | 0.766 | 0.703 | 0.645 | 0.592 | 0.544 | 0.500 | 0.460 | 0.424 |
| 10 | 0.905 | 0.820 | 0.744 | 0.676 | 0.614 | 0.558 | 0.508 | 0.463 | 0.422 | 0.386 |
| 11 | 0.896 | 0.804 | 0.722 | 0.650 | 0.585 | 0.527 | 0.475 | 0.429 | 0.388 | 0.350 |
| 12 | 0.887 | 0.788 | 0.701 | 0.625 | 0.557 | 0.497 | 0.444 | 0.397 | 0.356 | 0.319 |
| 13 | 0.879 | 0.773 | 0.681 | 0.601 | 0.530 | 0.469 | 0.415 | 0.368 | 0.326 | 0.290 |
| 14 | 0.870 | 0.758 | 0.661 | 0.577 | 0.505 | 0.442 | 0.388 | 0.340 | 0.299 | 0.263 |
| 15 | 0.861 | 0.743 | 0.642 | 0.555 | 0.481 | 0.417 | 0.362 | 0.315 | 0.275 | 0.239 |
| 16 | 0.853 | 0.728 | 0.623 | 0.534 | 0.458 | 0.394 | 0.339 | 0.292 | 0.252 | 0.218 |
| 17 | 0.844 | 0.714 | 0.605 | 0.513 | 0.436 | 0.371 | 0.317 | 0.270 | 0.231 | 0.198 |
| 18 | 0.836 | 0.700 | 0.587 | 0.494 | 0.416 | 0.350 | 0.296 | 0.250 | 0.212 | 0.180 |
| 19 | 0.828 | 0.686 | 0.570 | 0.475 | 0.396 | 0.331 | 0.277 | 0.232 | 0.194 | 0.164 |
| 20 | 0.820 | 0.673 | 0.554 | 0.456 | 0.377 | 0.312 | 0.258 | 0.215 | 0.178 | 0.149 |

| Periods (n) | Interest rates (r) | | | | | | | | | |
|---|---|---|---|---|---|---|---|---|---|---|
| | 11% | 12% | 13% | 14% | 15% | 16% | 17% | 18% | 19% | 20% |
| 1 | 0.901 | 0.893 | 0.885 | 0.877 | 0.870 | 0.862 | 0.855 | 0.847 | 0.840 | 0.833 |
| 2 | 0.812 | 0.797 | 0.783 | 0.769 | 0.756 | 0.743 | 0.731 | 0.718 | 0.706 | 0.694 |
| 3 | 0.731 | 0.712 | 0.693 | 0.675 | 0.658 | 0.641 | 0.624 | 0.609 | 0.593 | 0.579 |
| 4 | 0.659 | 0.636 | 0.613 | 0.592 | 0.572 | 0.552 | 0.534 | 0.516 | 0.499 | 0.482 |
| 5 | 0.593 | 0.567 | 0.543 | 0.519 | 0.497 | 0.476 | 0.456 | 0.437 | 0.419 | 0.402 |
| 6 | 0.535 | 0.507 | 0.480 | 0.456 | 0.432 | 0.410 | 0.390 | 0.370 | 0.352 | 0.335 |
| 7 | 0.482 | 0.452 | 0.425 | 0.400 | 0.376 | 0.354 | 0.333 | 0.314 | 0.296 | 0.279 |
| 8 | 0.434 | 0.404 | 0.376 | 0.351 | 0.327 | 0.305 | 0.285 | 0.266 | 0.249 | 0.233 |
| 9 | 0.391 | 0.361 | 0.333 | 0.308 | 0.284 | 0.263 | 0.243 | 0.225 | 0.209 | 0.194 |
| 10 | 0.352 | 0.322 | 0.295 | 0.270 | 0.247 | 0.227 | 0.208 | 0.191 | 0.176 | 0.162 |
| 11 | 0.317 | 0.287 | 0.261 | 0.237 | 0.215 | 0.195 | 0.178 | 0.162 | 0.148 | 0.135 |
| 12 | 0.286 | 0.257 | 0.231 | 0.208 | 0.187 | 0.168 | 0.152 | 0.137 | 0.124 | 0.112 |
| 13 | 0.258 | 0.229 | 0.204 | 0.182 | 0.163 | 0.145 | 0.130 | 0.116 | 0.104 | 0.093 |
| 14 | 0.232 | 0.205 | 0.181 | 0.160 | 0.141 | 0.125 | 0.111 | 0.099 | 0.088 | 0.078 |
| 15 | 0.209 | 0.183 | 0.160 | 0.140 | 0.123 | 0.108 | 0.095 | 0.084 | 0.079 | 0.065 |
| 16 | 0.188 | 0.163 | 0.141 | 0.123 | 0.107 | 0.093 | 0.081 | 0.071 | 0.062 | 0.054 |
| 17 | 0.170 | 0.146 | 0.125 | 0.108 | 0.093 | 0.080 | 0.069 | 0.060 | 0.052 | 0.045 |
| 18 | 0.153 | 0.130 | 0.111 | 0.095 | 0.081 | 0.069 | 0.059 | 0.051 | 0.044 | 0.038 |
| 19 | 0.138 | 0.116 | 0.098 | 0.083 | 0.070 | 0.060 | 0.051 | 0.043 | 0.037 | 0.031 |
| 20 | 0.124 | 0.104 | 0.087 | 0.073 | 0.061 | 0.051 | 0.043 | 0.037 | 0.031 | 0.026 |

Cumulative present value of 1.00 unit of currency per annum, Receivable or Payable at the end of each year for $n$ years $\frac{1-(1+r)^{-n}}{r}$

| Periods (n) | Interest rates (r) | | | | | | | | | |
|---|---|---|---|---|---|---|---|---|---|---|
| | 1% | 2% | 3% | 4% | 5% | 6% | 7% | 8% | 9% | 10% |
| 1 | 0.990 | 0.980 | 0.971 | 0.962 | 0.952 | 0.943 | 0.935 | 0.926 | 0.917 | 0.909 |
| 2 | 1.970 | 1.942 | 1.913 | 1.886 | 1.859 | 1.833 | 1.808 | 1.783 | 1.759 | 1.736 |
| 3 | 2.941 | 2.884 | 2.829 | 2.775 | 2.723 | 2.673 | 2.624 | 2.577 | 2.531 | 2.487 |
| 4 | 3.902 | 3.808 | 3.717 | 3.630 | 3.546 | 3.465 | 3.387 | 3.312 | 3.240 | 3.170 |
| 5 | 4.853 | 4.713 | 4.580 | 4.452 | 4.329 | 4.212 | 4.100 | 3.993 | 3.890 | 3.791 |
| 6 | 5.795 | 5.601 | 5.417 | 5.242 | 5.076 | 4.917 | 4.767 | 4.623 | 4.486 | 4.355 |
| 7 | 6.728 | 6.472 | 6.230 | 6.002 | 5.786 | 5.582 | 5.389 | 5.206 | 5.033 | 4.868 |
| 8 | 7.652 | 7.325 | 7.020 | 6.733 | 6.463 | 6.210 | 5.971 | 5.747 | 5.535 | 5.335 |
| 9 | 8.566 | 8.162 | 7.786 | 7.435 | 7.108 | 6.802 | 6.515 | 6.247 | 5.995 | 5.759 |
| 10 | 9.471 | 8.983 | 8.530 | 8.111 | 7.722 | 7.360 | 7.024 | 6.710 | 6.418 | 6.145 |
| 11 | 10.368 | 9.787 | 9.253 | 8.760 | 8.306 | 7.887 | 7.499 | 7.139 | 6.805 | 6.495 |
| 12 | 11.255 | 10.575 | 9.954 | 9.385 | 8.863 | 8.384 | 7.943 | 7.536 | 7.161 | 6.814 |
| 13 | 12.134 | 11.348 | 10.635 | 9.986 | 9.394 | 8.853 | 8.358 | 7.904 | 7.487 | 7.103 |
| 14 | 13.004 | 12.106 | 11.296 | 10.563 | 9.899 | 9.295 | 8.745 | 8.244 | 7.786 | 7.367 |
| 15 | 13.865 | 12.849 | 11.938 | 11.118 | 10.380 | 9.712 | 9.108 | 8.559 | 8.061 | 7.606 |
| 16 | 14.718 | 13.578 | 12.561 | 11.652 | 10.838 | 10.106 | 9.447 | 8.851 | 8.313 | 7.824 |
| 17 | 15.562 | 14.292 | 13.166 | 12.166 | 11.274 | 10.477 | 9.763 | 9.122 | 8.544 | 8.022 |
| 18 | 16.398 | 14.992 | 13.754 | 12.659 | 11.690 | 10.828 | 10.059 | 9.372 | 8.756 | 8.201 |
| 19 | 17.226 | 15.679 | 14.324 | 13.134 | 12.085 | 11.158 | 10.336 | 9.604 | 8.950 | 8.365 |
| 20 | 18.046 | 16.351 | 14.878 | 13.590 | 12.462 | 11.470 | 10.594 | 9.818 | 9.129 | 8.514 |

| Periods (n) | Interest rates (r) | | | | | | | | | |
|---|---|---|---|---|---|---|---|---|---|---|
| | 11% | 12% | 13% | 14% | 15% | 16% | 17% | 18% | 19% | 20% |
| 1 | 0.901 | 0.893 | 0.885 | 0.877 | 0.870 | 0.862 | 0.855 | 0.847 | 0.840 | 0.833 |
| 2 | 1.713 | 1.690 | 1.668 | 1.647 | 1.626 | 1.605 | 1.585 | 1.566 | 1.547 | 1.528 |
| 3 | 2.444 | 2.402 | 2.361 | 2.322 | 2.283 | 2.246 | 2.210 | 2.174 | 2.140 | 2.106 |
| 4 | 3.102 | 3.037 | 2.974 | 2.914 | 2.855 | 2.798 | 2.743 | 2.690 | 2.639 | 2.589 |
| 5 | 3.696 | 3.605 | 3.517 | 3.433 | 3.352 | 3.274 | 3.199 | 3.127 | 3.058 | 2.991 |
| 6 | 4.231 | 4.111 | 3.998 | 3.889 | 3.784 | 3.685 | 3.589 | 3.498 | 3.410 | 3.326 |
| 7 | 4.712 | 4.564 | 4.423 | 4.288 | 4.160 | 4.039 | 3.922 | 3.812 | 3.706 | 3.605 |
| 8 | 5.146 | 4.968 | 4.799 | 4.639 | 4.487 | 4.344 | 4.207 | 4.078 | 3.954 | 3.837 |
| 9 | 5.537 | 5.328 | 5.132 | 4.946 | 4.772 | 4.607 | 4.451 | 4.303 | 4.163 | 4.031 |
| 10 | 5.889 | 5.650 | 5.426 | 5.216 | 5.019 | 4.833 | 4.659 | 4.494 | 4.339 | 4.192 |
| 11 | 6.207 | 5.938 | 5.687 | 5.453 | 5.234 | 5.029 | 4.836 | 4.656 | 4.486 | 4.327 |
| 12 | 6.492 | 6.194 | 5.918 | 5.660 | 5.421 | 5.197 | 4.988 | 4.793 | 4.611 | 4.439 |
| 13 | 6.750 | 6.424 | 6.122 | 5.842 | 5.583 | 5.342 | 5.118 | 4.910 | 4.715 | 4.533 |
| 14 | 6.982 | 6.628 | 6.302 | 6.002 | 5.724 | 5.468 | 5.229 | 5.008 | 4.802 | 4.611 |
| 15 | 7.191 | 6.811 | 6.462 | 6.142 | 5.847 | 5.575 | 5.324 | 5.092 | 4.876 | 4.675 |
| 16 | 7.379 | 6.974 | 6.604 | 6.265 | 5.954 | 5.668 | 5.405 | 5.162 | 4.938 | 4.730 |
| 17 | 7.549 | 7.120 | 6.729 | 6.373 | 6.047 | 5.749 | 5.475 | 5.222 | 4.990 | 4.775 |
| 18 | 7.702 | 7.250 | 6.840 | 6.467 | 6.128 | 5.818 | 5.534 | 5.273 | 5.033 | 4.812 |
| 19 | 7.839 | 7.366 | 6.938 | 6.550 | 6.198 | 5.877 | 5.584 | 5.316 | 5.070 | 4.843 |
| 20 | 7.963 | 7.469 | 7.025 | 6.623 | 6.259 | 5.929 | 5.628 | 5.353 | 5.101 | 4.870 |

BPP LEARNING MEDIA

# Area under the normal curve

This table gives the area under the normal curve between the mean and the point Z standard deviations above the mean. The corresponding area for deviations below the mean can be found by symmetry.

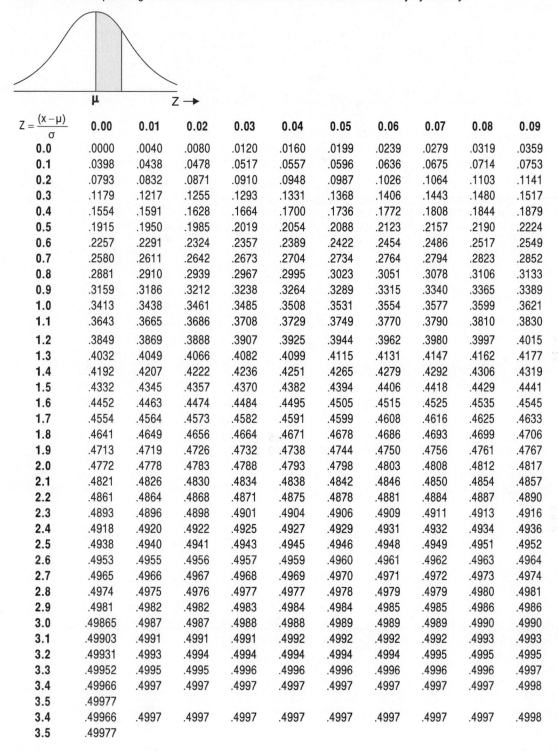

| $Z = \frac{(x-\mu)}{\sigma}$ | 0.00 | 0.01 | 0.02 | 0.03 | 0.04 | 0.05 | 0.06 | 0.07 | 0.08 | 0.09 |
|---|---|---|---|---|---|---|---|---|---|---|
| 0.0 | .0000 | .0040 | .0080 | .0120 | .0160 | .0199 | .0239 | .0279 | .0319 | .0359 |
| 0.1 | .0398 | .0438 | .0478 | .0517 | .0557 | .0596 | .0636 | .0675 | .0714 | .0753 |
| 0.2 | .0793 | .0832 | .0871 | .0910 | .0948 | .0987 | .1026 | .1064 | .1103 | .1141 |
| 0.3 | .1179 | .1217 | .1255 | .1293 | .1331 | .1368 | .1406 | .1443 | .1480 | .1517 |
| 0.4 | .1554 | .1591 | .1628 | .1664 | .1700 | .1736 | .1772 | .1808 | .1844 | .1879 |
| 0.5 | .1915 | .1950 | .1985 | .2019 | .2054 | .2088 | .2123 | .2157 | .2190 | .2224 |
| 0.6 | .2257 | .2291 | .2324 | .2357 | .2389 | .2422 | .2454 | .2486 | .2517 | .2549 |
| 0.7 | .2580 | .2611 | .2642 | .2673 | .2704 | .2734 | .2764 | .2794 | .2823 | .2852 |
| 0.8 | .2881 | .2910 | .2939 | .2967 | .2995 | .3023 | .3051 | .3078 | .3106 | .3133 |
| 0.9 | .3159 | .3186 | .3212 | .3238 | .3264 | .3289 | .3315 | .3340 | .3365 | .3389 |
| 1.0 | .3413 | .3438 | .3461 | .3485 | .3508 | .3531 | .3554 | .3577 | .3599 | .3621 |
| 1.1 | .3643 | .3665 | .3686 | .3708 | .3729 | .3749 | .3770 | .3790 | .3810 | .3830 |
| 1.2 | .3849 | .3869 | .3888 | .3907 | .3925 | .3944 | .3962 | .3980 | .3997 | .4015 |
| 1.3 | .4032 | .4049 | .4066 | .4082 | .4099 | .4115 | .4131 | .4147 | .4162 | .4177 |
| 1.4 | .4192 | .4207 | .4222 | .4236 | .4251 | .4265 | .4279 | .4292 | .4306 | .4319 |
| 1.5 | .4332 | .4345 | .4357 | .4370 | .4382 | .4394 | .4406 | .4418 | .4429 | .4441 |
| 1.6 | .4452 | .4463 | .4474 | .4484 | .4495 | .4505 | .4515 | .4525 | .4535 | .4545 |
| 1.7 | .4554 | .4564 | .4573 | .4582 | .4591 | .4599 | .4608 | .4616 | .4625 | .4633 |
| 1.8 | .4641 | .4649 | .4656 | .4664 | .4671 | .4678 | .4686 | .4693 | .4699 | .4706 |
| 1.9 | .4713 | .4719 | .4726 | .4732 | .4738 | .4744 | .4750 | .4756 | .4761 | .4767 |
| 2.0 | .4772 | .4778 | .4783 | .4788 | .4793 | .4798 | .4803 | .4808 | .4812 | .4817 |
| 2.1 | .4821 | .4826 | .4830 | .4834 | .4838 | .4842 | .4846 | .4850 | .4854 | .4857 |
| 2.2 | .4861 | .4864 | .4868 | .4871 | .4875 | .4878 | .4881 | .4884 | .4887 | .4890 |
| 2.3 | .4893 | .4896 | .4898 | .4901 | .4904 | .4906 | .4909 | .4911 | .4913 | .4916 |
| 2.4 | .4918 | .4920 | .4922 | .4925 | .4927 | .4929 | .4931 | .4932 | .4934 | .4936 |
| 2.5 | .4938 | .4940 | .4941 | .4943 | .4945 | .4946 | .4948 | .4949 | .4951 | .4952 |
| 2.6 | .4953 | .4955 | .4956 | .4957 | .4959 | .4960 | .4961 | .4962 | .4963 | .4964 |
| 2.7 | .4965 | .4966 | .4967 | .4968 | .4969 | .4970 | .4971 | .4972 | .4973 | .4974 |
| 2.8 | .4974 | .4975 | .4976 | .4977 | .4977 | .4978 | .4979 | .4979 | .4980 | .4981 |
| 2.9 | .4981 | .4982 | .4982 | .4983 | .4984 | .4984 | .4985 | .4985 | .4986 | .4986 |
| 3.0 | .49865 | .4987 | .4987 | .4988 | .4988 | .4989 | .4989 | .4989 | .4990 | .4990 |
| 3.1 | .49903 | .4991 | .4991 | .4991 | .4992 | .4992 | .4992 | .4992 | .4993 | .4993 |
| 3.2 | .49931 | .4993 | .4994 | .4994 | .4994 | .4994 | .4994 | .4995 | .4995 | .4995 |
| 3.3 | .49952 | .4995 | .4995 | .4996 | .4996 | .4996 | .4996 | .4996 | .4996 | .4997 |
| 3.4 | .49966 | .4997 | .4997 | .4997 | .4997 | .4997 | .4997 | .4997 | .4997 | .4998 |
| 3.5 | .49977 | | | | | | | | | |
| 3.4 | .49966 | .4997 | .4997 | .4997 | .4997 | .4997 | .4997 | .4997 | .4997 | .4998 |
| 3.5 | .49977 | | | | | | | | | |

BPP
LEARNING MEDIA